Copyrights and Trademarks for Media Professionals

Broadcast & Cable Series

Series Editor: Donald V. West, Editor/Senior Vice-President,
Broadcasting & Cable

Copyrights and Trademarks for Media Professionals

Arnold P. Lutzker

Focal Press

Boston Oxford Johannesburg Melbourne New Delhi Singapore

Library of Congress Cataloging-in-Publication Data
Lutzker, Arnold P.
    Copyrights and trademarks for media professionals / Arnold P. Lutzker
        p. cm. — (Broadcast & cable series)
    Includes index.
    ISBN 0-240-80276-4 (pbk. : alk. paper)
    1. Copyright—United States. 2. Trademarks—Law and legislation—
    United States. 3. Mass media—Law and legislation—United States.
    I. Title   II. Series.
KF2994.L88 1997
346.7304′82—dc21   96–52114
                                                                        CIP

British Library Cataloguing-in-Publication Data
A catalogue record for this book is available from the British Library.

The publisher offers special discounts on bulk orders of this book.
For information, please contact:

Manager of Special Sales
Butterworth–Heinemann
313 Washington Street
Newton, MA 02158–1626
Tel: 617-928-2500
Fax: 617-928-2620

For information on all Focal Press publications available, contact our
World Wide Web home page at: http://www.bh.com/fp

10 9 8 7 6 5 4 3 2 1

Printed in the United States of America

For Dad

Contents

Preface

We are in the midst of a media revolution. There are more ways for people to communicate than ever before—television and radio, cable and satellite, telephone and cellular, newspapers and magazines, the Internet. Each means of reaching an audience has one ultimate goal: providing viewers, listeners, or readers with content—news and information, entertainment and opinions. More than at any time in our history, the value of content has skyrocketed. Whether it is box office favorites, news reports of special events, reruns of TV sitcoms, home videos, or scribblings on e-mail, people covet the content they own and seek new outlets for releasing it. Thus, while the channels of communication are expanding, it is what's on those channels that reflects their ultimate value.

This book explains for those in the media and those who care about communications what they need to know about content. It takes the laws of intellectual property (IP)—copyright and trademark—and translates them into plain English. It helps answer those puzzling questions about what can be used on the air or in print and who really owns photographs, videos, storylines, and titles. With the publisher, Focal Press, we also offer readers a chance to follow new developments on a Web page. Look for us at: http://www.bh.com/fp/24080276.htm.

While these IP laws can be confusing, they are central to the media's effective operation. From program directors to advertisers, from scriptwriters to on-line access providers, from stringers to students, from home videocamophiles to Hollywood directors, the rules that we have set up to regulate the way we create and use content affect us all. Those on the front lines, whose jobs are to put programs and information together, are under the greatest stress. This book adds measures of understanding regarding the legal principles that shape our most precious commodity, the fruit of our intellect.

For creators and users of programming and content—which is just about everyone these days—the laws of copyrights and trademarks are the rules by which we organize the products of our intellectual efforts. These laws are challenged by an electronic system of communication that makes the ability to copy and disseminate, as well as to alter without a hint, simple and universal. At the same time, there are major realignments taking place among the owners of the media industries. Alliances between telephone and cable companies and acquisitions of television networks by movie studios are making current headlines. The passage of the 1996 telecommunications law reform has been lauded as one of the most significant legislative accomplishments of the Clinton administration. What are the economic forces driving these changes and how will they affect what we see and hear on the media? The pivotal element is content. With the knowledge you gain from this book, you will be better equipped to face the coming challenges in communications.

Part One

Copyright

Chapter 1

Overview of Copyright: The Big Picture

We begin with an overview of the texture of copyright. What is it and why should those in the media—those whose job is to *communicate*—have firm footing in copyright? Aside from an understanding of principles, our goal will be to impart information to help with judgment calls. Each story or report, every photograph or video, raises questions that touch on copyright. Because media communications are instantaneous and interactive, one cannot be paralyzed by the uncertainty about what can be used. So we will explain the traffic lights of the law—the green light that tells you when the road is clear to "go," the yellow light that urges "caution," and that red bugger that hollers "hold up, there's a problem here!"

What makes copyright fascinating from a legal perspective is that it involves the tension between two bedrock constitutional principles. Article I, Section 8, instructs Congress to pass laws granting to *authors exclusive rights to their writings for limited times*, while the First Amendment prohibits the Congress from passing laws that inhibit *free speech*. Copyright principles have been embodied in federal laws since the founding of our nation. Every 50 years or so, they have been updated to reflect technological developments, with the most recent major change coming in the Copyright Act of 1976. That statute has been amended several times since January 1, 1978, the day it took effect. The core principles of all these copyright laws have remained the same. The statutes

- Define what is meant by "exclusive rights"

- Set forth a term of years during which the "author" can commercially exploit the work
- Provide penalties for those who would take an author's work without permission
- Establish limited exceptions so that important public policies can be maintained

The tension with the First Amendment still persists, and in the age of cyberspace it is more acute. For example, how many times has it been said, "The Internet has no rules"? As this new medium evolves and electronic transmissions confront copyright barriers, the tension becomes palpable on the information superhighway. Rules of the road exist, but they are being challenged.

Traditional media—radio, television, cable, even the venerable newsprint—have had to grapple with copyright principles from their start. Even with decades of experience, confusion reigns in many quarters. "How far can one go in using the works of another?" is an age-old question. Let's put this in perspective by some "fact patterns." They have been drawn from my practice, and some of them may even sound familiar.

Setting the Stage

1. A radio manager had a long-running dispute with Arbitron. His station consistently paid a king's ransom price for the diary numbers. Fed up, he decides not to renew the ARB contract. As luck would have it, when the very next book is released, his station is credited with moving up five slots and is top rated in drive time. He has obtained a copy of the diary report from his ad agency, while highlights of the market numbers are printed in the trades. Determined to make a splash, his sales department prepares a chart based on the report, comparing the station's ARB ratings data with all competitors. The report is sent to 300 advertisers in the market. When ARB's rep calls to complain, the red-faced manager asks, "Any problem?"

2. A drama was caught on a videocamera by a viewer—police beating a drunk-driving suspect. The viewer called the station's "hotline" and a reporter picked up the videotape. It played on the noon news and by nightfall the network was clamoring for copy. The station sent it on, asking for on-air credit with its logo on screen at all times. When the viewer who made the tape saw his video on national television, at first he was thrilled; then, he got angry. Who gave them permission and where's my credit? He called his brother "the lawyer." Bro' contacted the station demanding big compensation. Does the viewer have a claim?

3. A Tennessee television station's fall campaign had a VOLUN-TEER theme. Every week for one year, the station produced five-minute pieces on the wonders of the state, from the statehouse to the mountain peaks. The series, which captured the native beauty of the countryside and the warmth of its residents, was scored with inspiring music from the Capitol Symphony Orchestra. The series was greeted with such acclaim that the station executives decided to market it commercially. They invested about $30,000 creating a two-hour video and released 5,000 copies to local chain stores. Their plans hit a snag when the Capitol Symphony Orchestra and some agents of the composers contacted the station. Is there exposure here?

4. Thanks to the retransmission consent rule in the 1992 Communications Act, stations could swap local carriage for a cable channel. With the popularity of regional sports networks, one station manager decided to capitalize on the wealth of local sports and to blend it with a mix of highlights pulled off regional cable channels. While camera crews went to high school and college fields taping games, station engineers edited video feeds pulled from other cable channels down to two-minute summaries. The station also hired former local sports stars to simulate play-by-plays by reading box scores from daily newspapers. How does this plan sound?

5. A rival television station had THE NEWS STORY OF THE YEAR breaking in its studio. A gunman, berserk but photogenic, stormed into Channel 5's studio with a loaded rifle. He demanded air time. The station executives had little choice but to oblige. What unfolded for the next hour was compelling, personal, and live TV. He ranted against his family, his city, his boss, his mindless life. Every television viewer in the market was riveted to the story. All the competitive stations could do was set their VCRs in motion, capture the drama, and wait for it to end. The conclusion was sad and horrifying—the gunman shot himself before startled onlookers. Instantly, the story was transformed into national news. When an arch competitor asked for permission to air its off-air tape of the events, Channel 5's News Director refused. Spurned but insistent, the rival station led its 6:00 p.m. newscast with the footage. Even after receiving a threatening call from Channel 5, the footage topped the 11:00 p.m. evening newscast. The next day, the lawyer's letter arrived. Concerned?

6. Breaking out of the crowded Internet pack requires creativity. One local phone company had a surefire campaign. It would build Web pages for all its customers and pick the "SWEET 7" each week, creating hotkeys for quick access to them. The home pages were creative and informative. Some enterprising subscribers placed newly released CDs by top recording artists on their Web sites. Others picked photos from *Time* and *Newsweek* and gave them new captions, while others scanned in chapters from bestsellers and rewrote the endings. The campaign proved instantly popular and subscriptions soared. The telco's Internet Access Group was sky-high until they received a letter from a publisher threatening a multimillion dollar copyright claim. What gives?

What is the common ingredient in all these stories? In each case, media outlets used content without regard to the consequences of copyright law. These are textbook examples of how to get into trouble with copyright—real fast. They also reveal the double edge of copyright. The content is tantalizing and useful. In each instance, there is a clear, discernible benefit that will flow from the use of the material. It may be that the harm to someone else's interest does not leap out at the users. But it should. There must be a calculation made, one that balances the attractiveness of using the content with the right to do so. That assessment is not measured simply by the urgency of delivering news or information, or a subscriber's desire for access. What must be assessed is whether the publisher has the *right to use* the content as planned. Could someone claim a superior right and stop the use? Must the content be cleared? Or can it be used, no matter what anyone says?

These are the copyright questions. Now, let's discover the answers.

Chapter 2

What Is Copyright?

The Constitution of the United States gives Congress power to pass laws to encourage authors to create works. The encouragement comes in the grant of exclusive rights to their writings for a limited time. Those rights are defined in the Copyright Act. There are only two key requirements to qualify as writings covered by copyright law. They are fixation and originality of expression.

Fixation

The work must be "fixed in a tangible medium of expression." Rules defining how a work is fixed are flexible. Over the years, they have adapted to new mediums. From piano rolls to computer disk drives, the law covers a broad swatch. Thus, the authors of books, articles, movies, tape recordings, snapshots, software, sheet music, newspapers, charts, graphs, choreography, and costumes can all lay claim to copyright protection in their works.

A glaring omission is unrecorded conversations. If words are not fixed, there is no copyright protection. However, flip on the tape recorder and, voilà, a fixation, and a copyrightable work. One of the most infamous conversations of recent years, Mark Fuhrman's private conversations about cops and blacks, were recorded without his awareness. The tapes, which debuted in the O.J. Simpson trial, are copyrighted works. Using them as evidence in a trial is one thing; exploiting them in the marketplace requires a copyright analysis. Had they never been recorded, the world would have lost an insight into the mind of a key witness. In addition, at some time in the future those tapes may have a publishing value. If the tapes are ever exploited, as they are *his* words, Mark Fuhrman will certainly have something to say about it.

When television was in its infancy, live performances were the norm. Some of these performances were preserved by kinescopes—recordings made off a monitor. The kinescopes qualify for copyright protection. Indeed, what we know about the early days of television, from "I Love Lucy" to "The Honeymooners" to "Today" and "Playhouse 90," is owed to those kinescopes. Some of those programs make up formidable parts of valuable cable networks such as Nickelodeon. Even without the kinescopes, many of the old TV performances had a copyrightable form—written scripts. Those scripts were fixed works.

Television's predecessor entertainment medium—vaudeville, with its stand-up comics—was notorious for "gag theft." The stars of the "Borscht Belt" regularly stole punch lines from each other. But they always did so with a copyright risk. If the gags were scripted, a copyright claim could have been made. However, if the live performances were ad-libbed and if no script or underlying text was used and no recording was made, then they would fall outside the scope of copyright protection. In sum, if a work is fixed in a tangible way, copyright law claims dominion over it.

Original, Creative Expression

Expressions come in different forms. They can be words contained in an article or a book; images preserved in photographs or film; sounds secured on sheet music, audiotapes, or CDs; or code stored on computer disks or hard drives. The list goes on. The other key for copyright law is that the fixed expression be *original* and *creative*.

Originality means the work is not copied; creativity means that it evidences at least a modicum of thought. Length is not crucial, unless it is simply too short, in which case trademark law takes over. However, string 15 to 20 words together and you have it. But—and this is important—you cannot reproduce another's work and claim protection for it. How much one can use the work of another, with or without permission, is a topic that will be addressed later. For the moment, it is important to understand that copyright protection comes into play when a work is original.

A copyright maxim that underlies the willingness of the law to protect original expressions is: *Expressions are protectible; ideas are not.*

For copyright law to merge with principles of the freedom of speech and the free flow of information, it is vital that ideas and facts not be owned exclusively by anyone. They are the building blocks of speech and knowledge. Thus, the fact that something happened—a crazed gunman took over a station, ranting for an hour and then killed himself—is available for anyone to explain, discuss, and put into *one's own words*. Copyright law defines ownership of those words.

The idea–expression dichotomy, as it is known, becomes more complicated when the photographic image that captures a moment or the narrative of the reporter on the scene embraces the essence of the event. Trying to put the expression into any other form may be difficult, if not impossible. The quintessential example of this statement is the Zapruder video of the assassination of JFK. That tape, shot by a bystander and later purchased by *Time* magazine, is a copyrighted work. But it is also the essence of a historic event. Can the visual retelling of that shooting be done *without visual quotations from the Zapruder tape*? An even more legally profound question from a First Amendment perspective is: *Should an author be prohibited from using the work without the consent of (and likely payment to) the copyright owner?* This question points to the core theology of copyright law—the economic incentives of encouraging copyrightable creativity—to which we will often return. For the moment, bookmark this question, because it is a vital part of the relationship of copyright law to the media, especially the news media.

A few years ago the U.S. Supreme Court had some things to say about the idea–expression dichotomy in a case involving, of all things, the telephone directory. The ruling, *Feist Publication v. Rural Telephone Service Co.*, now known as *Feist*, held that the names and phone numbers in the telephone books are "facts." Facts, as we know, are *not* copyrightable. Therefore, one could copy that information in the directories, without asking permission of the copyright owner of the telephone directory. The significance of the ruling was certainly substantial for the telephone industry. Yellow and white pages have proliferated. Today, CD-ROMs are sold with 100 million names and numbers. All that information is free for anyone to use. The fact that it was compiled by "the sweat of the brow," a previously respected basis for developing a copyright, became irrelevant, overnight.

For the media, this ruling has profound, yet uncertain, implications. When one's business is spending large sums to find facts and to be the first to report them, "ownership" of those facts becomes vital. As employees of media outlets in a highly competitive business, managers want the public to see it first on their station, in their newspaper, on their outlet. The race to develop facts, assemble them, and attract a regular audience is what the business is about. However, if facts are unprotectable, then guarding information and exploiting it prudently requires great care. Incorporating sufficient expression in the story overcomes the dilemma, at least from the copyright perspective. If one's facts are replete with expression, then copyright law will protect you. For example, what appears to be "facts," let's say, the Nielsen overnight ratings, is often more complex from a copyright law point of view. The entire market report, which allocates shares among stations based upon application of complex research data and statistical analyses, constitutes Nielsen's opinion about relative shares. There is nothing inevitable about the results, and another researcher might reach a different result, even with identical raw data. Thus, those rating reports are copyrightable, even though they represent one entity's attempt to define the "facts" of the viewing marketplace. Just how *Feist* will work its principles on this and other media issues will be one of the great copyright stories yet to unfold.

There are three other introductory concepts that should be explained—the public domain, copyright formalities, and publication.

The Public Domain

Here's a concept that is full of confusion! Public domain works, by definition, are not covered by copyright. They are free to use and reuse. In some cases, they are easy to identify. Remember what was said at the start. The founding fathers empowered Congress to grant exclusive rights to works for *limited times*. In copyright terms, this means decades, not centuries. From 1909 to 1977, the copyright term was 28 years, but it could be renewed for an extra 28 years if some formalities were followed. The current copyright law grants protection for the period of the life of the author plus 50 years, or 75 years in the case of works not owned by a person. Just as the term was extended in the 1976 copyright reform, modern copyright advocates want it extended again; this time for an extra 20 years to match some rule changes in Europe.

Whatever the limit, at some point in time, the term of copyright protection will expire. So, for example, in the case of an individual creator who dies in 1997, all works of that person will enter the public domain by 2048. For already published works owned by corporate entities, count back 76 years to locate works that are no longer protected by copyright law. If the term is extended an extra 20 years to 95 years, or life plus 70, the owners get a bonus period during which to exploit the work exclusively. (Here's a *yellow caution light:* Unpublished works have a different time rule, which will be discussed below.)

The limited term is why many of the great works of 19th century literature, for example, Mark Twain, Melville, or a current favorite, Jane Austen, are exempt from copyright protection. The authors were entitled to exploit those works during the copyright term, but now they are freely available to be copied by others in their original form or adapted to new media. But bear in mind, however, *new matter is entitled to a new copyright term.* Indeed, changes can transform a public domain work into a protectable copyrighted work. For example, a movie based on a book has its own term of protection. The storyline may be as old as the ages, but the photography, dialogue, music, costumes, scenery, and direction all raise new copyright claims.

Many television stations have received notices from distributors who claim to be selling "public domain movies." Rather than pay nasty license fees, these folks provide lists of films that they claim are free of any copyright restraint. With the rising cost of licensing films, these circulars can be pretty tempting. In some cases, they may even be correct. There are many films, which for reasons that defy commercial logic, were not protected as they should have been. Although copyright law permitted the owners to keep the works under the full scope of legal protection, administrative lapses or downright carelessness permitted the work to drift into the public domain.

When station managers—or personnel with any media outlet—receive notices about these works, before acting, they should do some homework to determine if, indeed, the work is in the public domain. The benefits of this research can be substantial. With the exorbitant costs of securing broadcast rights for programming, obtaining quality public domain works, which retain their broadcast appeal, can fit the bill when stations are looking to reduce expenses.

However, the need to do homework must be underscored, because many of the works touted as public domain are not. And some works that used to be public domain may have been resurrected by clever entrepreneurs. A favorite illustration of this point could be found at the NAPTE (National Association of Program Television Executives) shows of some years ago. NAPTE is *the* broadcast syndication trade show. Vendors of new and old programs sport their stuff there for television affiliates seeking programming products.

One enterprising executive had discovered that the old Basil Rathbone *Robin Hood* films were in the public domain. The copyright owner of the movies failed to meet the renewal requirement and the movies' copyrights lapsed. This executive had a plan. By adding some new score to the old films, he was able to obtain a new copyright for the derivative work—the public domain (p.d.) film with the copyrighted music. Thus, even though the principle of public domain meant that the films could be copied or broadcast by any media company without paying a license fee, the new music could not be copied or performed without the executive's consent. While a few original prints of the public domain films were floating around, the newly scored copies contained an updated copyright notice. Unless the broadcaster could secure a copy of the original, there was no way of knowing what was new material and what was old. The executive, who trouped around NAPTE dressed à la Robin Hood and his merry men, made a modern morality tale with a twist—he took from the rich (the original movie producer) and gave to the poor (himself).

In addition to works for which copyright has lapsed, works of the federal government are exempt from copyright protection. The federal government, which is funded by tax dollars from all citizens, is not entitled to copyright protection by statutory decree. This means that many works, such as government films produced by the military filmmakers, reports released by federal agencies, and photographs taken from U.S. satellites, may be copied.

Even with a clear statutory dictate, however, there is a cautionary note to interject. If the government works were made under contract with a nongovernmental entity or individual, then the contract covering the creation of the work may transfer the copyright interest to the independent contractor. This crucial limitation, which can wreak havoc with plans to use governmental works, is often misunderstood. So it bears repeating and absorbing. *If the actual creator of a work published by the U.S. Government is not an employee of the government, that creator may have a legal claim to copyright in the final work.* For example, footage of U.S. troops landing during the Persian Gulf War shot by a cameraman accompanying the forces looks like a government work. However, if the photographer was not in the U.S. military, but rather was a private photographer hired to accompany the men, then that video may be used by the government, but it is owned by the photographer. One would have to review the contract between the military and the individual to know for sure.

With contracts like these generally inaccessible, what's a media maven to do? First of all, look at any notices that are published with the footage. Is there a copyright notice, and if so, in whose name is it? Is there any other legend associated with the tape? Assuming that information is not available, recall how the tape was obtained. Was it released to the media during a press briefing and by whom? Was it downloaded from a channel, and if so, whose? Was there any accompanying printed text? Doing your copyright homework is a necessary chore.

Formalities

Copyright law used to be laden with *formalities*. This was a relic of the English law tradition from which U.S. copyright standards developed. For almost two centuries, American copyright proprietors had to follow the rigors of the system or risk losing all of a work to the public domain. Thus, formalities such as *notice and registration after publication* had strict requirements. Disobey at one's peril.

Today those requirements have all been eliminated, a byproduct of the U.S. Government's decision to join the Berne Convention in 1988. Berne, the leading international copyright treaty, defines the terms by which its members must live and provides copyright rules in their countries. While there is flexibility (so-called national treatment) in a number of situations, the Berne Convention resolves that the copyright owner should not be subject to formalities in order to enjoy copyright rights. Thus, in 1988 U.S. copyright law finalized a process begun in 1976 to strip the law of formal requirements in order to smooth the way for entrance into a key part of the international copyright community. This is not to say that prior to 1988 the United States was not already a world copyright leader. Indeed, it was *the leader*. Moreover, by other multicountry and bilateral treaties, the United States had copyright relationships with most of the industrialized world. But the Berne Convention offered special legal access for U.S. copyright proprietors, especially owners of films and software, enabling them to attack directly the growing problem of international copyright piracy, the commercial theft of their copyrighted works.

For those steeped in copyright traditions prior to 1978, the formalities of U.S. laws were among its enduring and distinguishing features. Indeed, for users and owners of copyrighted works, formalities offered vital information. Since publication required notice of ownership, one could tell who claimed ownership of works created before 1978 simply by looking for notice. Works published without notice risked being thrown into the public domain. Similarly, registration was required "promptly" after publication. While courts ultimately saw fit to give the term *prompt* the generous meaning of the initial copyright (28 years), formalities retained an ability to affect the legal status of works. As explained in the discussion on public domain, careful research can yield proof that the works are free to use.

However, copyright law comes with some tricks to salvage even works thought to be public domain for many years. For example, the Frank Capra classic, *It's A Wonderful Life*, became a Christmas season staple when its copyright lapsed—the owner forgot to follow the formality of renewal. The movie *fell into the public domain*! However, an enterprising film distribution company, Republic Pictures, recently claimed that it held the copyright to the *underlying script for the film* and that telecast of the film without its consent is copyright infringement. Strange as the result may seem to many, this is sound copyright theory. Legal precedent has held that the copyright in the underlying script, from which the film is derived, is a separate copyrighted work. Even if the copyright in the film has lapsed, the owner of the underlying story may claim rights to the film as a derivative work. For broadcasters, caution may be necessary next time they decide to air this special film. A check with your copyright lawyer will tell you whether Republic Pictures has succeeded in enforcing its claim.

Publication

When copyright law was updated in 1976, Congress merged all copyright principles into a unitary federal system. In the process, it eliminated the notion of "common law copyright." Prior to this reform, if a work was unpublished it could remain the exclusive property of its owner and his or her heirs *forever*. The critical dividing point was publication. When a work was sold, loaned, licensed, or given away, the law deemed the work published and subject to all the formalities of federal law. An entire body of copyright law interpreting the instance of "publication" evolved because the dividing point between published and unpublished works had dramatic legal consequences.

One important copyright rule is that "performance" is not defined as publication because no copy changes hands. Hence, live concerts are not publication of a musical score. By analogy, when broadcasting began to impact copyright law, it was ruled that a telecast was not a publication of a work. If copies were sold or given away, that would constitute a copyright publication. But the mere airing of a program on radio or television did not constitute publication. Thus, all the old network radio shows, which were telecast live in many cases, with recordings made simultaneously, did not constitute published copyrighted works. This means that a body of works for which copyright registration was not secured remained under common law copyright protection. Only if tapes of the shows were distributed would the program cross the copyright divide. At that point (but prior to 1978), failure to follow the formalities created the potential that the work could fall into the public domain. Complying with the formalities meant that the owner was entitled to claim the benefits of federal copyright for the work during the years it was protectable.

While elimination of formalities has diminished the legal significance of publication, the concept still has important consequences. First of all, when the law was reformed in 1976, common law copyrights were given a federal term of protection. Even though they may have been created a century or more before, the term of copyright protection for unpublished works was extended at least to the year 2002. If they are published between 1978 and 2002, the term will last at least until 2027. Thus, for a vast body of unpublished works, including private manuscripts, photographs, letters, etc., here is the cautionary point to understand: Even though the works are very old, for example, dating back to the early 1800s, they could still be owned and subject to full federal copyright protection.

There is a related copyright doctrine called *first sale*. The core idea is that the law gives the creator of works the right to choose the forum of first publication. In general, the courts have been very solicitous of the copyright owner's right to choose the first release of a work. If a work has not been published and someone wants to exploit it before the owner, the copyright law plants a red flag signaling: Wait a second! Almost always, the owner will be able to stop the use.

This principle can catch not only the unsophisticated, but also the experienced. A few years ago, Random House, one of the nation's leading book publishers, prepared a biography of reclusive author J.D. Salinger. In the book, many private letters written by Salinger were to be published for the first time. Even though Random House and its author came by the letters lawfully, the legal issue they faced was whether the book could be published against Salinger's express opposition. Anticipating substantial sales based on advance publicity, Random House had a huge run in its first edition. To Random House's dismay, Salinger sued for injunctive relief, demanding on copyright grounds that the publication be halted. And the court agreed with him. Through appeals, Random House learned that its case was a loser, a victim of common law copyright and the first sale doctrine. Because Salinger's letters were unpublished, the court reasoned that they were entitled to a higher degree of protection. The First Amendment rights of Random House's author, who sought to bring new insight into the literary hermit, suffered in comparison with Salinger's first sale rights to his private letters. Even though someone else owned the physical paper on which his words were written, the copyright to those words remained with Salinger. Random House had to destroy the books in its inventory. Many years still remain before Salinger's rights will be extinguished.

The rights of J.D. Salinger to first sale of his words offer a useful transition. It is now time to move from a general discussion of the principles underlying copyright law to the rights themselves.

Chapter 3

The Copyright Rights:
The Coin of Copyright

What *precisely* do we mean by copyright? The copyright law sets forth five exclusive rights of owners. They are as follows:

1. The right to reproduce the work
2. The right to prepare derivative works based on the original
3. The right to distribute copies to the public
4. The right to perform the work publicly
5. The right to display the work publicly

To copyright purists, these rights are expansive and embrace every conceivable way in which works can be copied. Thus, as technology has revolutionized modern communications, copyright has kept pace. Whether it is radio and television, photocopy or fax machines, the Internet or transnational digital satellite signals, copyright law applies.

These rights and all exploitation associated with them are within the exclusive province of the copyright owner. They represent economic gold, the coin of copyright, because they can be sold, licensed, or loaned for a fee. They can also be given away for nothing. These rights define copyright interests. They also set parameters: If a third party wants to use another's copyrighted work in a way not embraced within these rights broadly defined, then copyright law may not apply.

This principle is at the focal point of a current debate to which we will return: Whether transmitting copyrighted works via e-mail or the Internet is an exempt private distribution or a public transmission, and thus a copyright infringement. Some courts have already ruled that unauthorized electronic transmissions via bulletin boards are copyright infringements; however, there is sufficient uncertainty in the interpretation of "public distribution" that copyright owners have supported amending the copyright law to make it clear that transmissions are public distributions.

Now, let's take a closer look at these crucial copyright rights.

The Reproduction Right

The reproduction or copying right is what most people think about when copyright comes to mind. The ability to control copying is the signature of the act. Copying can be done in different formats, and copyright law has something to say about each type. Traditionally, copying was literally grabbing a pencil and paper and writing down what someone else wrote. When technology advanced, it became the ability to record by film, tape, and photocopy machine. In today's digital environment, the copying issue has become rarefied. It is easy to understand that duplicating a floppy is copying, and so too is storing a work on a hard drive. However, when a computer is turned on and a working copy is entered into a computer's random access memory (RAM), that too is a reproduction, albeit a temporary one. Indeed, the copyright law was modified in 1980 to ensure that a licensee or owner of a software program has the right to put that computer program into his or her working files without violating copyright law. It's a simple concept, and one that is essential to the smooth operation of technology, but it still required an act of Congress to accomplish the result.

In broadcasting, there is an analogous issue, the "ephemeral copy." When radio stations play music, it is often necessary to make a copy of the tape or disk in order to permit smooth access for on-air play. Stations that promise "ten hits in a row, with no commercial interruption" prepare the tapes in advance so they can mix and match songs and themes. These stations, which are licensed by performing rights societies—the largest of which are American Society of Composers, Authors and Publishers (ASCAP), Broadcast Music Inc. (BMI), and the Society of European Songwriters, Authors and Composers (SESAC)—to perform works, are not separately licensed by those societies to reproduce them. However, the Copyright Act offers an option. It allows broadcast stations licensed to perform music to make ephemeral or short-term use copies to facilitate their transmitting activities. We'll have more to say about music rights issues in broad-cast in a later chapter. For now, it is sufficient to understand that the copyright law allows responsible, but limited, use of those copies.

The Derivative Works Right

Under copyright law, once you create a work for one medium, your rights extend to all media. Adaptations, translations, updating, and sequels—all are embraced within the derivative copyright. The para-digm example is a successful book that has many incarnations. The author of the book holds rights to all its progeny—a movie, a play, a television series, a video game, a theme park ride, a book on tape, a sequel, posters, note cards—the list goes on and on. Oftentimes, the book itself is derived from a shorter piece, such as an article, treat-ment, or poem. Like a precious jewel, a successful copyrighted work has many cultural surfaces. Copyright law allows the author to claim each side of creativity.

But even as the derivative right offers the copyright owner mul-tifaceted entitlements, residing in the jewel is a copyright flaw: the idea–expression dichotomy. While the preparation of a derivative work exclusively belongs to the owner, if a third party only takes the "idea," and then creates a distinct work, copyright law will not find fault. In the media, this translates into the honored art of catching up with the leader. When CBS had the hit series "Dallas" capturing view-ers every week, ABC came along with "Dynasty." Different characters and plot, but a similar idea—prime time, one-hour soap, with money and fabled families at the core.

When the movie *Twister* opened to long lines and public fascina-tion in the summer of 1996, local television newscasts began running reports on violent weather, while some movie studios were racing to develop themes about natural catastrophes. To take the Michael Crichton book and replicate it would violate the derivative right. However, taking the theme of scientists chasing weather phenomena and creating an original work borrows only an idea. If the new work is invested with novel expression, it is copyrightable.

Public Distribution Right

For most of American copyright history, until 1978, copyright law was a two-part system. There was common-law copyright and federal copyright. The dividing point was "publication." If a work was published, it was subject to federal controls and granted a copyright term embracing a limited number of years. If it was unpublished, it could be owned by its author forever. Public distribution was a legal synonym for copyright publication.

The statute defines "publication" as a distribution of copies to the public or other transfer of ownership by means of sale, lease, loan, or otherwise giving away copies of a work. Offering copies to a group of people for further distribution, public performance, or public display also qualifies. Thus, the ability to provide a single work to a multiplicity of people, even if no money changes hands, constitutes public distribution. Good Samaritans, who believe the world would be better off if people could receive free copies of video or software programs, violate copyright law, even though they do not profit, because they are wrecking the legitimate, public distribution market of the copyright owner.

This issue has reached a boiling point in the world of electronic communications. Copyright owners are so nervous about the capacity of new technology to create perfect digital copies of original works and the mind-set of ardent advocates of freeware on the Internet that they have pushed Congress to look closely at the copyright rules in the electronic world. The single most important goal is to enshrine the principle that any transmission or electronic communication is a public distribution. The implication of this principle is significant, not only for digital transmissions, but for all kinds of communications.

Public Performance Right

There is no copyright right more central to broadcasting and cable than the public performance right. Everything these media do involves performing works for the public. While there may or may not be copies made of works (as a practical matter, virtually all content, even live telecasts, is recorded in some fashion), all programs are sent out over the airwaves or by wires to a public audience. These transmissions constitute public performance.

For the media, it means that copyright clearances are the protein of its life system. Knowing that the broadcasting station has the right to transmit programs to the public is essential to operation. Acquiring interests that fall short of public performance means that the ability to telecast is in question. Due to the breadth of material used on the air and the fact that public performance rights to the various elements of a program may be held by many parties, it is necessary to ensure that all pertinent copyrights have been cleared. This may be a tedious task, but it is vital to the smooth operation of all media.

The public performance of a work also occurs in face-to-face environments, such as in a nightclub, concert hall, convention hall, or at a street fair. The copyright law fully embraces the delivery of works by individual speakers, as well as musicians and performers, in all public settings. In fact, any rendition before an audience in a public place or beyond a normal circle of family and friends is covered.

While describing the public performance right it is useful to mention three related concepts. First, copyright law makes it clear that performance is not distribution. The cases that developed this maxim predated video recording devices; nevertheless, the concept is sound. Merely performing a work for the public in no way means that the public is entitled to retain a copy of the work. Conversely, being allowed to perform a work publicly does not mean that one holds the right to give copies of that work to others. As a result, ubiquitous warnings against copying accompany many telecasts, such as baseball games ("No reproduction, distribution, or use of the telecast may be made without the express written consent of Major League Baseball"), or are displayed in theaters ("No still photographs may be taken of this performance"). From a copyright perspective, this suggests that the public performing entities may not hold the additional rights to distribute copies or to prepare derivative works. In simple terms, the right to perform does not ensure the right to distribute copies. The media must approach any request from the public to make copies of telecasts with great care.

Second, let's distinguish "performers' rights," from "public performance right." Under copyright law, the people who deliver the work to the public in a performance, in particular, the actors and actresses, or the musicians and the singers, do not hold copyright to their performance. This means that even though the people who wrote the words and the music for all compositions aired on the radio are entitled to copyright royalties whenever their songs are performed (these are the funds that the music performing rights societies— ASCAP, BMI, and SECAC—collect for their members), there is no comparable statutory right for the singers and musicians. While their contracts may allow them a spot of revenue whenever their rendition of the work is performed on the air, most often that is not the case.

Periodically, there is talk in Congress about amending the copyright law to extend rights to performers. This movement is receiving new attention because of interest in the international sphere for such protection. At some point in time, the performer's right and the rights of all who participate in the making of works may be better defined. For the time being, however, the performer's right to his or her rendition of a work should be seen as an area of potential expansion of copyright law.

Finally, there is the notion of a performance right in sound recordings. We will have more to say about this issue in our discussion of musical content in broadcasting, but, briefly, record label companies have long claimed they deserve royalties when their recordings are played publicly. Copyright protection for these companies is only a relatively recent development (1972). When their rights were added to the law, no public performance right was granted. A debate over this issue rages in Congress, made particularly acute by the ease of copying digital works.

Right to Publicly Display

Placing works in public places for people to view is a time-honored raison d'être of museums. For many in the media, the display right was ignored. The computer revolution has changed all that. Public display takes on new meaning in the digital world. When electronic transmissions are received on computer screens, the operative principle is that they are displayed. The question that arises in cyberspace is whether such displays are "public" and whether the copyright law has any basis to control them.

We have already mentioned the flexibility of copyright law to adjust to new technology, and to define certain uses and practices as coming within the scope of recognized rights. However, the question posed by digital transmissions, which are directed to individuals on their private computers, is whether the transmission, once received, constitutes a "public display." Certainly, it is a far cry from an Andy Warhol painting hanging in the local museum.

In sum, these are the copyright rights. They are statutory defined grants, which means that they are creatures of our legal system. In a world where the intellectual property of the United States is one of the hottest commodities of commerce, these rights are the building blocks for exploitation. Other nations define them differently, but thanks to international treaties, most of the elements of U.S. law are replicated all over.

The copyright rights, however, come with a string attached. Attached to each right, attached to each work, are a series of exceptions or limitations. These qualifications are the way the law reconciles copyright principles of exclusivity and economic exploitation with competing public interests, such as free speech, library and educational entitlements, and the complex needs of cable television and public broadcasting. Let us turn our attention to these limitations.

Chapter 4

Limitations on Copyrights: The Chili Pepper of Copyright

If all the copyright law did was grant rights to authors, our task would be simple. Since any copying would require permissions, one would always have to identify the owner of the copyright and seek approval to use even small portions of a work. However, while the grant of rights is broad and quite inclusive, there are a series of statutory limitations to those grants. Within the parameters of these limitations, there is much play and much confusion. Some of these exceptions were written expressly for the media. In all, they represent the chili pepper of copyright law, which creates the spicy intellectual mix.

Fair Use

The most important limitation in copyright law is fair use. Fair use is a defensive claim, which can negate a charge of infringement. It provides that in the course of "criticism, comment, news reporting, teaching, scholarship or research," one can use a copyright work without the consent of the owner. To determine whether the use is indeed fair, four factors are considered. They are:

1. The purpose and character of the use, including whether the use is for commercial or noncommercial purposes
2. The nature of the copyrighted work
3. The amount and substantiality of the portion used in relation to the work as a whole

4. The effect of the use on the potential market for or value of the original

While these criteria are deceptively simple, they have been the subject of more copyright litigation than any other limitation in the law.

Fair use does not have a bright-line test. Because analysis of the legal criteria will vary with the facts of each case, one cannot know with absolute certainty whether the fair use assertion will be sustained. The real hitch, however, is that as a defense to a claim of infringement, one has by definition infringed a copyright and is left to then justify the activity. This uncertainty can be both an advantage and a curse. Due to the way copyright penalties are meted out, if a copyright owner challenges a use and loses, the owner could be forced to pay the fair user's legal fees. Therefore, owners must exercise reasonable caution when a responsible fair use claim is involved.

As a handy reference for understanding the limitation, let's think of a baseball park, which we'll call "The Field of 'Fair Use' Dreams."

The statutory exemption defines the parameters or the ballpark in which fair use is played. News reporting, comment, criticism, research, scholarship, and teaching are the field of play. For the media, most of its core activities come within these terms; thus, its activities are favorable ones for a fair use analysis.

But being in the ballpark does not mean that using another's work is fair. To make that judgment, one must consider the four criteria—the bases within the ballpark. You cannot claim fair use unless you successfully touch all the bases. So let's focus in on these four criteria:

First Base: Commercial/Noncommercial Use

This factor assesses the economic motivation involved in the *exploitation*. For some time it was thought that any commercial use would doom the likelihood of winning a fair use argument. However, more modern interpretations provide that while a noncommercial use is favored, a commercial use is not fatal to a fair use claim. Nevertheless, to the extent that the use is not directly tied to a commercial activity, the user has a better chance of prevailing. By definition, public (noncommercial) television stations have an easier time establishing fair use than their commercial counterparts. Similarly, if the use is part of a product that is sold to the public directly for a fee, it is harder to prevail. In baseball terms, this factor affects the speed with which one circles the bases such that the swifter runner may make it home while the slower runners may be cut down.

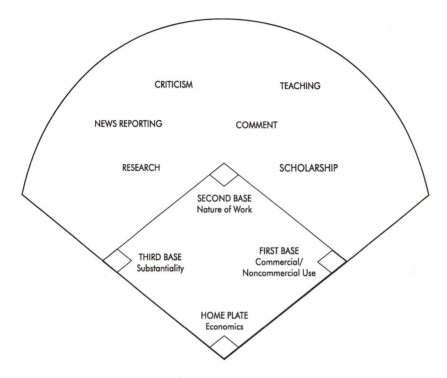

Figure 4.1 The Field of "Fair Use" Dreams

Second Base: Nature of the Work

This factor is one that looks at the copyrighted work being used. The more expensive the original copyrighted work was to produce, the more available licensing of the work may be and the more commercial exploitation may be made of the work by the owner, the less likely a fair use will be found. For these reasons, one needs to understand the economic marketplace for copyrighted works. For example, movies are among the most expensive copyrighted works to produce. The average box office feature costs close to $50 million to produce and distribute. Copyright owners try to recoup every dollar, and the law discourages taking from those works. Conversely, works that are cheap to produce, that have long exhausted their market, and that have limited value are fairer game. In between lies the vast bulk of current copyrighted works for which claims of fair use hinge on an analysis of the final two factors.

Third Base: Substantiality of the Taking

How much can you safely take from another's copyrighted work? The best advice always is: as little as necessary. While it has been said that there are few original ideas these days, the goal is to borrow only what you must in order to create your own new work. In some instances, taking the whole work is hard to avoid. A photograph, a short poem, a one-paragraph news article, these are all tempting targets, and it is often hard to make do with less than the whole. In the copyright analysis, substantiality is measured in relation to the entirety of the original work. The mathematics can be crucial. Judges will count words, minutes, inches, and then form their own opinion about the fairness of the taking.

A rule of thumb is take no more than five percent of the original work. The chances of winning against an irate copyright owner are greatly improved when the taking is less than five percent. While a few courts have ruled that 25 to 50 percent may be fair use in some cases (and even 100 percent, in the case of a photo), the danger zone is clearly marked in red when you take more than 25 percent. Taking 5 to 25 percent of the original leaves you in a yellow zone, where other factors come into play.

However, even the five percent test has its limitations. In one of the most significant fair use rulings, *Harper and Row Publishers, Inc. v. Nation Enterprises (Nation)*, the U.S. Supreme Court held that the use of just 300 words out of a 200,000-word book constituted "unfair use." The reasons were severalfold: the book, the memoirs of former President Gerald Ford, featured a first-person narrative by the man who pardoned President Richard Nixon. President Ford and his publisher had a magazine serialization deal with *Time*, which promised a preview of the work a few days before formal release. Relying upon a purloined copy, *The Nation* magazine published the part of the book that contained Gerald Ford's own description of that pardon. So even though the percentage was about as low as you can go, 0.0015 percent, the use was considered to be *the heart of the book*.

Moreover, *The Nation* scooped not only the publication of the book, but it beat *Time* magazine to publication. Since one of the bedrock copyright principles is that an author has the right to determine the time and manner for "first sale" of a work, *The Nation's* audacity in scooping the author left the court very reluctant to find fair use.

As a result of the *Nation* decision and the case involving J.D. Salinger's letters, it had been thought that a winning fair use claim could never be made if the work in question was unpublished. However, in 1992 Congress amended the fair use provision to explain that fair use could apply even to unpublished works. Nevertheless, it remains very difficult to prevail on a fair use claim if the original is unpublished, even where only tidbits of the original work are taken. Now, assuming that you have made it as far as third base, the hardest part is still to come.

Home Plate: Economics of the Taking

Copyright interests are economic rights in works. Perhaps the most important factor in assessing fair use is: What is the impact of the use on the market for and value of the original? If the answer does not damage the economic interests of the copyright owner, you may round the bases and get home safely.

The economic impact has two tests: (1) Has the value of the original work been diminished? and (2) Has the owner been deprived of just economic rewards? We must bear in mind that most uses have some economic impact. It is often argued in copyright infringement cases that the user has "benefited" the copyright owner by making the work more popular, giving it broader exposure, or opening new markets that the owner did not tap but that are now ready for exploitation. That argument, while sounding fine, has been stated by those who never made it to home plate.

There is an obvious relationship between the economics of the taking and the first test—commercial or noncommercial use. It is easier for those claiming noncommercial status to argue that they have not profited by the taking. However, to the extent the user generates any funds (for example, even a public broadcasting station may raise donations), then the taking can have economic impact. Moreover, the failure of the copyright owner to exploit a market is not a sound argument. Just as the law allows the copyright owner to market the work, it allows the owner to withhold the work from a market until he or she is ready. If that time never comes, that is the owner's decision. Remember, unpublished works are still protected by copyright law.

The economics of the taking are also closely tied into the issue of substantiality. The less that is taken, the stronger the claim that the user's product is what is attracting the market, not the portion of the original work. If only a snippet of a film or book is copied and constitutes only a tiny part of a new work, then it is hard for the original owner to assert either that the infringing work relies for content on the original or that its own marketplace has been severely damaged.

Well, there you have it. A round-tripper. Touch every base success-fully and you can score, using someone else's work without permission or fee. However, fail to touch each base or overslide any one of them, and the claim of fair use will fail. When we discuss damages and remedies in the next chapter, you will appreciate how costly a mistake that can be.

Educational Limitations

Libraries, archives, educators, and public broadcasting are given modest leeway to conduct their public purposes while making use of copyrighted works of others. Some of the limitations were the product of intense negotiations between copyright interests and these public-spirited institutions. Nevertheless, the narrowness of their scope suggests an important caution: If copyright proprietors will fight hard to limit the exceptions for educational institutions, the private exploitation of copyrighted works will be even more restricted.

Library Photocopying and Lending

Born out of the advent of twentieth century photocopy technology and in the wake of a unique split on the Supreme Court (a decision that ended in a four-four tie with one justice abstaining), Section 108 of the Copyright Act attempts to explain how one can use the copier in a library without paying dearly for the privilege. The provision is divided into three parts: copying for preservation; copying for scholarship, research, and private use; and loaning copies of works.

The first principle is that libraries can duplicate works in danger of being lost due to age or condition, but only if the copies made are for preservation, not for resale. The second precept is that the copies can be made available to the public, provided that they are done on a single-copy basis and the library has no knowledge that the duplicated works will be resold. The libraries are instructed to post copyright notices near photocopy machines, advising the public about the limits of the law. Finally, libraries are free to publicly lend copies of works they own to others. This is a corollary of the "first sale doctrine." Although the copyright owner can control when a work is published, the copies are owned by the buyer, who is free to loan or resell such copies.

Copyright law recognizes a distinction between copies and copyrights. One can buy and own a copy of a book, a video, or a record. That physical copy can be resold or given to anyone else. If it becomes rare or if it increases in value, the possessor of the copy can keep the appreciation. Owning a copy, however, does not translate into owning copyrights. The five statutory copyrights belong only to the author.

In short, the library limitation makes it clear that while individually owned copies of works can be circulated without violating the exclusive distribution rights of the copyright owner, there is no right belonging to the holder of the copy to make widespread use of the copy.

Public Broadcasting

Under the Copyright Act prior to 1978, certain nonprofit uses of copyrighted works were exempt from any liability. As nonprofit activities expanded dramatically in scope in the 1950s and 1960s, pressure mounted to modify the free ride for nonprofits. However, the copyright compromise of 1976 left certain limitations on owners' rights intact.

One of the industries that has benefited from special treatment is public broadcasting. In a provision that tries to strike a balance, Section 118 of the Copyright Act allows public broadcasters (as defined in the Communications Act) on the one hand and copyright owners of musical works and published pictorial, graphic, and sculptural works on the other hand, without fear of antitrust laws, to negotiate a "voluntary license" allowing the radio and television outlets to perform, display, and produce works incorporating the copyrighted material. However, if voluntary licenses are not agreed to, then the copyright law provides that a government entity (originally the Copyright Royalty Tribunal, and now the Librarian of Congress) can set royalty rates. In practice, voluntary licenses rarely materialize, so every year the Library of Congress reviews the government mandated rates and makes adjustments. Payments from the stations go to the owners. The public broadcasting exception does not cover the use of movies or nondramatic musical works, or the production of a program drawn to any substantial extent from a published compilation of pictorial, graphic, or sculptural works. If unlicensed by the copyright owner, uses would be controlled by fair use rules.

Performance Exemptions

One of the most hotly debated issues in copyright law is the appropriate limitation on the performance right. The heat generated by this issue is due in part to the fact that performing rights licensing societies are strong and cohesive. ASCAP (American Society of Composers,

Authors and Publishers), BMI (Broadcast Music, Inc.), and SESAC (Society of European Songwriters, Authors and Composers) represent the vast majority of people who write popular songs and lyrics. They are tenacious in their efforts to sign up licensees, and under special legal rules they are allowed to offer licenses not only for individual works, but also for all the works in their repertoire, the so-called blanket license.

Although prior to 1978, nonprofit entities, including educational institutions and public broadcasters, were free to perform copyrighted works, the 1976 reform act struck a new balance in Section 110. The limitations set forth in this provision allow the performance of all kinds of works in classroom settings. Face-to-face teaching has a broad exemption for performing works without requiring any permissions. When works are transmitted from a classroom setting to another locale, however, some constraints are set forth on the unlicensed use of works. Most significantly, audiovisual works (movies and videos) are excluded. Further, the transmission must be made primarily for reception in places devoted to instruction.

The transmission of courses outside of a classroom, an updated version of the "Sunrise Semester" television show of the 1950s, is at the heart of the larger legal issue of "distance learning." The more that classroom transmissions have the look and feel of television programming, the more copyright owners require that any use of their works be cleared at the source and resist the claim that they are subject to unlicensed exemptions. The debate is coming into clearer focus and will be hotly contested in the next few years.

Another performance exemption that has been the subject of U.S. Supreme Court opinion and legislative reform is the playing of radio and television signals in commercial establishments. Since anyone can play a radio station in one's own home, should there be any limit if you want to keep the radio on for background music on the job? Since the performing rights societies have licenses to cover background music, their answer has always been: "Get a license." However, Section 110(5) of the Copyright Act allows small store owners to keep a radio on as long as the equipment used is similar to that found in a home, no charge is made to hear the transmission, and the broadcast is not tampered with.

To explain the exemption, courts have clarified what is meant by "equipment similar to that used in one's home." At base, no more than four speakers can be hooked together, and the square footage of the store must be less than 2,000 square feet. In short, the owner of a downtown department store cannot play a radio station's music throughout the building and claim an exemption. If you want to play that station, you must get licenses from ASCAP, BMI, and SESAC.

Beyond these performance exemptions, the Copyright Act details a host of other instances where publicly performed music is exempt from copyright liability, principally in the context of religious services, governmental meetings, state agricultural fairs, nonprofit veteran and fraternal organization functions, music stores, and transmissions to the blind. These limitations are detailed and, when these issues arise, the precise language of the statute should be consulted to confirm that the exemption applies.

A word of caution should be added here. Radio stations may be drawn into the middle of performance exemption disputes. A local merchant who advertises on the station may ask for permission to carry the station's programming free of charge. It is always tempting to keep the advertiser happy. However, the radio station's license with ASCAP and BMI does not allow the station to grant the rebroadcast right without regard for the copyright interests of the folks who wrote the music. A station may authorize anyone to perform works the station owns, but it cannot encourage retransmission of licensed material without clear authorization. When these questions arise, the station should exercise care in making sure that it has the right to do what is asked, or else just say no.

A similar problem arises when a station's programming is used by businesses for telephones put on hold. Even though it seems innocuous, a radio station may not have authority to grant a local business the right to play the station when the business phone is on hold. The performing rights societies have licenses specially drafted to cover this situation. If a station is asked for permission and grants it, despite the absence of a clear right to do so, it may be liable to the copyright societies for contributing to the infringement of the performance right. Therefore, any such request should be carefully considered, and consent be clearly limited to programming owned by the station. At the same time, the station should refer the enterprise to the performing rights societies for music clearances.

Cable and Satellite Compulsory Licenses

Compulsory licensing is a creature of the copyright laws. It is a government-mandated loan of copyrighted material in exchange for a governmentally fixed fee. No "free marketplace," but a marketplace nevertheless. The theory of compulsory licensing is that the marketplace is so unwieldy and technology so pervasive that public policy must reconcile these competing interests to allow consumers access to the copyrighted works.

When copyright law came face-to-face with content-eating technology, such as cable television and satellite-delivered programs to home dish receivers, complicated compromises were devised. The compulsory licenses for the cable and satellite industries qualify as winners of the Blue Ribbon of Complex Federal Law. We will discuss the rules in depth in Part Four: Content and New Media. For now, it should be understood that at the core of these rules is the principle that copyright law will not stop the technology. Congress found a way to require fees to be paid by the cable and satellite resale carrier industries for the privilege of delivering programming to paying subscribers, without having to navigate the maze of negotiated clearances.

Compulsory Music License

The granddaddy of compulsory licensing traces back to the 1909 Copyright Act. The license for making and distributing sound recordings has a simple premise. Once a composer has published a musical work, others should be allowed to record their interpretation for play on mechanical devices by paying a fixed fee. Thus, after Liza Minnelli introduced "New York, New York," Frank Sinatra was able to make his own version of it. To qualify, Mr. Sinatra and his recording company either had to negotiate a mechanical license or, failing agreement, to take the compulsory route by filing a notice of intention to obtain a compulsory license with the copyright owner of the musical work. Then, a royalty had to be paid for every record, tape, or CD distributed to the public, based on the greater of a certain number of pennies per recording or a smaller number of cents per minute of playing time. It is paid directly to the copyright owner on a monthly basis. The rates may change periodically, so it is necessary to check on the current rule.

A key restriction is that the use must be for a recording that will be sold to the public for private use. This compulsory fee does not permit the public performance of the music of another. Either the performer or the venue must obtain a performance license when rendering a work to the public.

Sound Recordings

Just as the compulsory license for making and distributing records does not sanction public performances, it also does not allow someone to duplicate the original sound recording and sell copies to the public. In the 1960s and early 1970s, the arrival of the tape recorder to the mass market spurred a booming, albeit underground, business in selling bootleg tapes. The tapes, copies from purchased originals, were sold on the street for one-half or less the price in the retail stores. Some clever bootleggers even registered with the copyright owner under the mechanical license of the 1909 Act and used a gap in copyright law that did not provide express protection for sound recordings. The underlying works (music and lyrics) were protected, but the actual LP or tape was not.

Despite the absence of legal protection under copyright, the U.S. Supreme Court in *U.S. v. Goldstein* found that the duplication violated local laws of "misappropriation." In other words, it was theft. The bootleggers were stymied. The practice drew such attention that Congress amended the Copyright Act, effective February 15, 1972, to make sound recordings separately protectable. The owners of sound recordings, however, were not granted the five copyrights of other owners. Owners of sound recordings were only granted the right to control copies, preparation of derivative works, and public distribution.

The failure to acquire "public performance" rights in sound recordings has remained a contentious issue between the record manufacturers and broadcasters. Major record labels have pressed Congress for changes in copyright law to require that when a sound recording is played in public, not only are the composer and lyricist entitled to royalties, but the owner of the record itself also deserves some revenue.

Voicing the contrary view has been the broadcast industry. To the radio and television industries, which pay huge license fees to perform music, a performance right in sound recordings would be another big charge with little benefit. The stations argue that the record labels receive bounty enough from the commercial sales that follow air play. To the record labels, those sales are welcome, but why not get extra compensation from a blanket license fee, like the composers and lyricists do?

The battle lines have been drawn even more tautly with the advent of digital sound recordings. The copyright interests in the music industry have pressed very hard for a copyright interest in the public performance of digital sound recordings. They argue that due to the superior ability of digital technology to copy music off the air, once digital sound gains a dominant market share, home taping will replace buying CDs. While home taping with older technology is enshrined, the digital domain offers a new opportunity to revise the rules.

There appears to be an inevitability about the argument. In 1992, Congress passed what could be the precursor legislation, amending the Copyright Act and establishing a royalty system covering the sale of digital audio recording devices. As a result, DATs (digital audio tape machines) and other digital devices are subject to a tax at the source, a flat royalty of $1 or two percent of the transfer price for every machine initially distributed in the United States. The money collected is distributed to those whose works are included in digital recordings. Two thirds of the royalties are placed in a Sound Recordings Fund, with most of the money going to producers of sound recordings, but with four percent reserved for nonfeatured musicians and vocalists. The remaining third is placed in a Musical Works Fund, to be split between music publishers and writers.

Ephemeral Recordings

One of the well-used media limitations under the copyright law is the ephemeral recording exemption. By this arrangement, radio stations do not have to perform a needle drop on every selection performed. They are allowed to prepare a prerecorded tape of songs to be played, making for a smooth, easy-to-follow program, without running afoul of the copying right. The rule, however, applies only to "transmitting organizations" entitled to broadcast music to the public under a performing rights license. Without that safety net, there is no ephemeral exemption. Furthermore, the ephemeral recordings prepared for the transmitting organization must be (1) retained and used solely by the transmitting organization that made it, (2) used solely for its own local transmissions or for archival purposes, and (3) destroyed six months after the public use or archived.

The rule has occasionally been stretched to the limit by music format distributors, who tape songs in order to license precisely organized formats, such as beautiful music, oldies, MOR, and rock. Since so many aspects of the music business have been subdivided and licensed for copyright purposes, these distributors have escaped the scrutiny of the licensing sources. Nevertheless, the practice fits the mold of a use that requires clearance, even though the habit of the industry is to ignore it.

Chapter 5

Remedies for Infringement: Paying the Price

Failure to comply with the rules of copyright can be very expensive. The law lays out a number of penalties for misuse of copyrighted works. Most importantly, there are money damage claims that courts will enforce. The costs of noncompliance can be profits and actual damages. But sometimes these values are difficult to determine. To ensure that the copyright owner is compensated when works are infringed, the law establishes "statutory damages," which may be sought in lieu of the others. Statutory damages are fixed at $500 to $20,000 per work infringed. If the actions of the infringer are willful, these claims can balloon to $100,000 per work.

A copyright owner does not have to offer any proof of loss to claim statutory damages. That makes them a powerful remedy and a key disincentive to infringement. Once the determination has been made that there is an infringement, the owner chooses which form of monetary remedy to seek. For media users who violate copyrights, the statutory claim can have a multiple effect. Since damages accrue to each *work infringed*, if a number of works are involved, statutory claims can be sought for each work.

For example, when the right of a satellite resale carrier to retransmit broadcast signals under the cable compulsory license was tested in court, the carrier was well aware that every day about twenty programs were delivered to cable systems. Thus, every day statutory damage claims accrued at the rate of $10,000 to $400,000! Similar exposure could occur if a telephone company decided to deliver off-the-air signals to the public without clear entitlement under the Copyright Act's compulsory licensing limitation. If disputes linger in courts while the alleged infringing activities continue, the statutory claims could be monumental.

Despite the windfall from statutory damages, even claims of actual losses can be huge. In the digital arena, film distributors and recording companies are frightened that copyright pirates can cause tens of millions of dollars of losses simply by posting copyright works on the Internet, thus allowing millions of people access to them. With digital copying as easy to accomplish as pushing a few computer keys, their fears are well-founded.

In addition to monetary damages, the copyright law provides that infringement can be stopped and the infringing goods seized and destroyed. In a case of media copying appropriately known by the call letters *WPOW*, when a broadcast applicant was found to have copied the engineering section from a competitor's file, a court ordered the purloined portion deleted from the infringer's application. The result was potent—POW!—the stripped-down file was held to be incomplete and the application was summarily dismissed.

Injunctive relief is vital when infringements occur at formal checkpoints, such as customs depots. In the world of satellite communications, the capacity to enjoin the transmission is essential to maintaining control over the work because the transmissions may be unstoppable once sent.

As a rule, injunctive protection proves more complex in on-line environments. With the anonymity that often is associated with on-line and Internet communications, it is cumbersome to locate and stop infringers. Even if a targeted infringing site is shut down, clever hackers can move to another location to continue illegal postings. Cyberspace offers the greatest challenge yet to the efforts to stop infringing activities.

Another dynamic feature of copyright remedies is that the prevailing party in a copyright lawsuit can seek to be reimbursed for legal fees and expenses. In the U.S. judicial system, where parties typically pay for their own lawyers and where the costs of bringing a case can be so high that some rights are never enforced, this provision makes copyright law very accessible to owners and, therefore, a credible threat to would-be infringers. It means that if one risks infringing copyrights and is successfully sued, the cost could include paying the fees of all the lawyers in the case, which is not a happy thought.

There are some important limitations to be aware of in the case of the statutory damages and attorneys' fees provisions. First, if the owner is a U.S. resident or citizen, the work must be registered with the Copyright Office at the time of the infringement. Even though the old formality of registration was made permissive by the 1976 reform and cannot be required of any foreigner claiming rights under the Berne Convention, for U.S. nationals the requirement can still have vitality. The balance struck encourages filing works with the Copyright Office by requiring that prior to filing a lawsuit, registration for the work must be perfected.

Second, there are two exceptions to the principle that infringements occurring prior to registration do not subject the defendants to statutory damages or attorneys' fees. One exception is the case of infringements occurring very soon after publication, as in the case of live transmissions, such as a baseball game or daily newscast copied simultaneously with its telecast. In that event, the owners have three months to register and still claim the special statutory benefits for infringements dating from the initial telecast. The second exemption is for works of foreign nationals. No formality can impede their rights.

In the absence of compliance with these rules, infringements will still allow the owner to seek actual damages and accounting of profits, but the other benefits would be lost. Bear in mind, however, that if the infringements are continuing, statutory entitlements are reestablished each time the infringing behavior is repeated.

Third, there are some exceptions that apply to qualified nonprofit educational institutions (such as libraries and public broadcasters) and innocent publishers. If the qualified nonprofit user has reason to believe that the use of the work was allowed under the fair use doctrine, the court should omit any statutory damage claim. There is still exposure to actual damages, but the special bonus allowed by copyright law would be unclaimed against those defendants.

For "innocent" publishers, which may include a broadcaster carrying advertisements containing copyright infringement materials that it had no reason to believe were unauthorized, the law limits damages to $200.

This gives you an idea of the costs of missteps that attend copyright infringement. Since all media are voracious when it comes to content, the potential for large claims to develop is substantial.

Chapter 6

Ownership of Copyright: Keeping What's Yours

In an era when content is prized as an asset of commerce, the claim to ownership of copyrighted works becomes more intense. Therefore, care must be taken in establishing the lineage of works. Failure to attend to the niceties of ownership could destine the careless to headaches or, worse, the loss of rights. The most practical moment to address these matters is *before the work is created*. Devise a plan for the ownership of a work and do your homework.

There are a handful of important points to know about owning copyrights. First, a basic concern relates to meeting the statutory requirements for creating a work, including fixation in a tangible medium. Second, perhaps the central issue of ownership involves the rules of authorship, and most particularly the relationship between employer and employee. Third, there is the matter of acquiring or transferring rights. Fourth, registration and term of copyright should be underscored. Finally, know your friendly agency—the Copyright Office. Now, let's take a closer look at the ownership manual.

First, Creating the Work

We have already discussed the fact that the rights of a copyright owner come into being only when an original work is "fixed in a tangible medium." As noted, the concepts of "originality," "fixation," and "tangible medium" are fluid. Originality involves sufficiency (fifteen words or more, for example) and no direct copying. The fixation requirement is satisfied when the work is preserved, even if it is later erased or destroyed. As to "tangible medium," almost any environment will do—paper, tape, disk drive, piano roll, film, negatives, microfiche, even steel. As long as one can point to the object where the fixation occurs, copyright rights are assured. About the only thing that would not constitute copyrightable medium is conversation, unless, of course, it is recorded.

Second, Authorship

Copyright rights belong to authors. The author of the copyrighted work is the one who created it. Sometimes, the author is an individual, such as a poet or sculptor. Other times, the author is a team of creators, such as in the case of a song, where one party writes the score and the other the lyrics. When the creation is joint, copyright law acknowledges the capacity of works to have more than one author. If their contributions are inseparable, then each may lay claim to the entire work and be entitled to all the benefits of ownership in that work. However, in that instance, the joint owner owes a duty of accounting to the other if the work generates income.

When works are created by employees in their jobs, the copyright is usually owned by the employer. "Work for hire" is a time-honored copyright principle that allows the person or entity paying for the work to enjoy the economic benefits of the effort. If a number of creators are involved in the development of a work for an employer, then it makes sense to concentrate the copyright interests in a single party to facilitate exploitation of the work.

For example, movies or television programs are described as a collaborative art form because there can be dozens of individuals who combine to create them. When you see the credits roll, there are many people who individually created copyrightable elements, which have been merged into the final picture. Directors, cinematographers, writers, set decorators, costume designers, even the performers, can each lay claim to copyrightable elements.

Typically, the producer has each of these people sign a contract that grants the producer control of all the copyrights and related interests, such as rights of publicity and the authority to make sequels. The signing of the contracts is important because in many instances the producer does not employ these individuals in the traditional sense; they are not on staff but are hired for the specific project. At the conclusion of their work, these artists move on to another job, often with a different producer. Under these circumstances, these employees are independent contractors.

The copyright law is specific that if the individual is not regularly employed, there should be a "writing" indicating that his contribution to a work, such as a motion picture, is a "work for hire." In the absence of this magic language, the individual may claim a right to copyright, which could seriously impact the way in which the rights of exploitation are implemented.

When an individual works for another and one's job is to create a copyrighted work, the employer owns the product. Since most people are employed by corporations or others, more often than not the ownership of copyright rights does not belong to the individual creator. Any employee whose job is to create works becomes disenfranchised from his or her creations. But the copyright bargain is that they are paid for their labor.

Sometimes the bargain becomes complicated to sort through because the job that one is hired to perform may not cover the creation of the specific work. For example, the sales manager at a television station who is encouraged to write a treatment for a new sitcom or to develop a jingle for a new station theme is not employed as a scriptwriter or composer. Unless the creative task is within the employee's "scope of employment," he or she is the author for copyright purposes. If the plot is marketable or the theme a hit, it is owned by the employee, not the boss.

However, if the task is within the scope of employment, the employer has a reasonable claim to ownership. In the case of the jingle, it may be argued that the assignment is part of selling the station. Of course, things could be simplified by making sure that the employment agreement covers the creation or is modified to accommodate it.

Matters become more ticklish if the creator is an independent contractor. The general rule is that a non-employee hired to create a work, such as an outside software developer hired to create a program to manage a cable company's subscriber database, owns the product. Unless there is a written contract that gives the end product to the firm that is paying the bill, the result is uniformly in favor of the independent contractor and may be a nasty surprise to the employer.

As it turns out, software development has been particularly contentious in many industries, including the media. If the software works, there may be annual fees to pay for maintenance or upgrades and, most likely, it cannot be used by sister companies without express permission. Many misunderstandings are created when the paying party does not realize that although it may have footed the bill to develop the copyrighted software product, paying the fee does not transfer copyright ownership. Remember, the right to use a copyrighted work does not always equate with the right to own it.

Third, Acquiring and Transferring Copyrights

As companies are bought and sold, their assets, including their authorship of copyrights, trade as well. The media merger activity of the 1990s was driven by a desire to lock in control over not only channels of distribution but also the elements of content. With every acquisition proposal, however, there must be a careful researching of the employment agreements and outside contractor relationships to be certain that the assets of the parties are what everyone believes them to be.

When the Copyright Act was changed in 1976 to create a unified federal system, it made clear that copyright rights were divisible. An owner could license more than one party to the rights, and could separate the rights and divide them any way he or she pleased. The right to control making copies could be granted to one party and the right to control public performance to another. This is quite common in the music industry, where the performing rights societies ASCAP, BMI, and SESAC are authorized to grant public performance in songs but are not allowed to grant synchronization rights, that is, the right to copy works onto video.

Intellectual property, like real estate, can also be passed to heirs. In fact, the effort to extend the term of copyright from fifty to seventy years after the death of an author (from seventy-five to ninety-five years in the case of entities) is principally designed to allow great-grandchildren of authors to obtain the benefit of their efforts. The children and grandchildren had been protected by the fifty-year term, but the change would enable an additional generation to reap the economic fruits of creativity.

One special limitation on assignment in the copyright rules is intended to help the struggling artist who prematurely in life has to part with his or her work. Under the termination of assignment, the heirs of an artist who assigned a creation can cancel the assignment in the thirty-fifth to fortieth years, provided the original creator is dead. This rule only benefits the widow or widower, children, and grandchildren. Its intended effect is to restore some of the balance that might not have existed when the original transaction was completed.

Fourth, Registration and Copyright Term

Copyright registration rules had been a fixture of the U.S. system. However, in 1978, mandatory registration was eliminated as we began to adopt a Berne-compatible legal system. Under Berne, no formality, neither registration nor notice, can interfere with a copyright owner's full enjoyment of rights. So registration, a system whereby every work had to be filed with the U.S. Copyright Office promptly after publication, was eliminated in favor of a permissive filing system. Copyrights could not be conditioned on filing with the Copyright Office.

Registration, it must be said, is a good thing. Since it is often necessary for users to track down copyright owners to seek permissions, registration affords a simple and effective mechanism to know when works are published and who owns them. If copyrights are transferred, the assignment can also be noted. Even though we now have a permissive filing system, registration remains important for several reasons:

- Many copyright owners file for every work. It is sound business because it allows the world to know how to reach you. That can be important when rights are being sought or when people want to contact the right person when works are used, even on a fair use or other permissive basis.
- For U.S. citizens, it is necessary to file if rights are to be enforced. And, if registered at the time of an infringement, the copyright owner may claim statutory damages and attorneys' fees for infringing acts that occurred after registration.
- The practice of registering assignments of rights allows the public to track down current owners. Orphaned copyright works is a serious problem in the field of preservation and archiving. In particular, creators of photographs are often unidentifiable because the works have no source on them. Since a registered work must have a copyright notice identifying the author and the year of publication, it contains two key bits of data that allow for identification of the right parties in interest.

Renewal of copyright deserves a mention as well. Under the rules in place from 1909 to 1977, published copyrights were protected for twenty-eight years, once registered. To claim a second twenty-eight-year term, a renewal application had to be filed. If the owner forgot to file, or concluded that the work did not merit it, the copyright fell into the public domain. Some famous works, including the movie *It's a Wonderful Life* met this fate. No amount of wishing can resurrect lost copyrights. Even though the copyright term was extended by the 1976 reform, if a work was first published under the 1909 Act, Congress required that a renewal be filed in the twenty-eighth year to claim the additional twenty-eight years, plus an extra nineteen (thus providing a total of 75 years). However, as it developed, so many well-intentioned copyright owners forgot or did not know about the renewal requirement that many works were being dedicated to the public domain without any plan to do so. That situation was rectified when Congress ended the renewal requirement altogether in 1992.

The Constitution allows Congress to grant copyrights for a "limited term." In our history, the term of copyright has been extended many times. In 1978 the term of copyright increased from twenty-eight years, with a renewal term of twenty-eight years (for a total of fifty-six years), to the life of the author plus fifty years or, in the case of works owned by entities, such as corporations, seventy-five years from creation. Works in their original or renewal term were protected for seventy-five years, and works that were never published, and therefore existed only under common law copyright (which was to last forever), were granted an automatic term to 2002. If they are published before the end of 2002, the term extends to 2027.

Once the term of a work expires, even if the government later extends the term for copyrights, there is no resurrection, with one exception. To satisfy international pressures when two important treaties were signed in 1994, Congress amended the copyright term rules. Thanks to copyright law amendments adopted after GATT (General Agreement on Tariffs and Trade) and NAFTA (North American Free Trade Agreement), if the copyright for the work of a *foreigner* (this rule applies only to non-U.S. citizens) who did not comply with a U.S. copyright formality was lost, following Copyright Office procedures the copyright could be restored for the balance of the full copyright term. Thus, anyone relying on the public domain status of foreign works is cautioned to check out the restoration lists kept by the U.S. Copyright Office.

COPYRIGHT TERM SHEET

- 1909–1977: 28 years, plus renewal for another 28 years.
- 1978: Life of author plus 50 years or in the case of works owned by entities—75 years from creation.
- Tack On: As of 1978, all works still in their 1909 term get an extra 19 years protection.
- Unpublished works: Copyright until 2002; if published between 1978 and 2002, term extended until 2027.
- GATT/NAFTA Resurrection: Public domain works of foreign citizens may be restored to balance of their original terms if the loss of copyright protective status in U.S. was due to failure to comply with formalities.

The generosity of our system was jolted recently when many European countries decided to extend their copyright term to the life of the author plus seventy years, or ninety-five years for entities. In order for American copyright interests to receive full credit in these foreign states, principally in Europe, our law has to be changed to add twenty years to the term, making it "life plus seventy" or ninety-five years. A drive to extend the U.S. term was launched in 1995.

Originally, the term extension bill was deemed a sure lock at passage. But the bill became embroiled in copyright debates unrelated to term, such as (1) the obligation of bar and restaurant owners to pay copyright fees when satellite signals are played in the establishment, (2) the duty of television and radio evangelists to pay music license fees, and (3) the impact of the changes on libraries that wait for the copyright term to expire so that they may freely use many dated but scholastically important works.

Whether or not the term extension passes before this book goes to print, it is a reasonable bet that the longer term will be the international rule very soon and the United States will join with the other leading copyright nations of the world.

Fifth, the Copyright Office

The agency that supervises this system is the Copyright Office. It is a user-friendly agency that processes the registration of all works and retains copies of these works in the archives of the Library of Congress. It has a host of informative reports and documents that make copyright life less complex. One thing it does not do, however, is issue advisory opinions applying and interpreting copyright law to facts, such as whether a use is a fair use. The Copyright Office also collects compulsory royalties and supervises arbitration panels.

As recipient of copies of published and unpublished registered works, it is a rich treasury of American history, and its officers serve as special advisors to Congressional Committees on copyright policy in public and private forums. When a 1996 bill proposed to merge all the Intellectual Property (IP) agencies (Patent, Trademark, and Copyright Offices) into a new super-independent organization, there was a huge outcry against moving the Copyright Office out of the Library of Congress. The motion had few public supporters. Thus, it remains a part of the Library and the legislative branch.

We have presented the broad framework, the outer layers of law, and its practical applications. Now it is time to approach another wing of IP rules important for media content—trademark law. Once you have a grounding in the philosophy of this sister body of rules, you will be in a position to appreciate the shading and nuances necessary for true understanding of media copyrights and trademarks.

But before we do, let's summarize the core premises of copyright law:

CORE OF COPYRIGHT

1. Authors are entitled to exclusive rights in their works for limited times.
2. The copyright rights are broadly defined to cover copying in any format, creating derivatives, and publicly performing, displaying, or distributing a work.
3. The rights are subject to crucial exemptions, including fair use, compulsory licensing, and educational uses.
4. The law provides powerful remedies to enforce the rights.
5. There are no longer any prerequisites to claiming copyright; the original work only has to be fixed in a tangible medium.
6. The term of copyright is for an author's life plus fifty years (seventy-five years if an entity).

Part Two

Trademarks

Chapter 7

What Is a Trademark?

While copyright law defines the rights and responsibilities regarding "works," trademark deals with the subtle arena of words, names, phrases, and symbols. In many ways, these linguistic and visual elements are the linchpins of relationships in the media. Serving as source identifiers, trademarks allow the consumer to relate to a product or service based on a body of experiences. They are most fundamentally distinguished from copyrights by their length. While copyright law requires the element of originality and generally applies to works of at least 15 words, trademarks can be short and pithy. One word like "Paramount," a string of letters like "ABC," a short phrase like "All the News That's Fit to Print," a visual design like the CBS "eye," or sounds like the melody of "When You Wish Upon A Star," all constitute trademarks. They identify a source and embody a reputation.

Thus, television sets that come from "GE," movies from "Universal," Internet access from "MCI," and cable services from "TCI," all have meaning to the public. While the consumer relies upon the information to help make choices in the marketplace, the trademarks also serve as the identity of the enterprise or individual. Investing in trademarks is a way of defining who and what a media business is all about.

Sometimes, marketplace competitors, searching for an advantage, play off the reputation of others. Whether by comparison advertising or tricks to simulate logos, trademark issues dominate the efforts of many who seek to create a niche in the media market. Being savvy about trademarks is essential to the smooth operation of any media enterprise.

Before delving into the key issues of trademark law, let us take a look at the principal concepts that underlie this discipline.

Trademarks, Service Marks, Trade Names, and Trade Dress

While we will use the word *trademark* to refer to all the types of elements, there are actually four terms that need to be distinguished. A *trademark* is a word or phrase that is physically on a good or attached to a label on a good. When the product is tangible, the legal term is *trademark*.

A *service mark* is the word or phrase associated with the provision of services. You cannot touch a communications service, but you know the firms that deliver those services by these symbols. MCI, AT&T, WTBS-TV, Time-Warner, and KABC-AM are all service marks for the entities that provide communications services. It is, of course, possible that the same symbol may serve as a trademark and a service mark. While in the phrase "AT&T long distance services," "AT&T" is a service mark, when you reach for an "AT&T telephone," the letters function as a trademark.

In terms of legal treatment, there is no difference whatsoever between trademarks and service marks. Although this was not always the case, and in some instances in international law there remain some differences, the practical effect for U.S. law is semantic.

Semantics would not characterize their difference with *trade names*. A trade name is an individual's or a company's actual business name. A business trade name is readily identified by additional words, such as "Company," "Corporation," "Ltd." and "Inc." Trade names often come attached to addresses and phone numbers.

Unlike trademarks and service marks, which linguistically are adjectives, describing a type of good or service, trade names are nouns, identifying a particular person or business. A trade name can be converted into a trademark, such as "AT&T, Inc." provides "AT&T telephone services." The subtlety of the distinction can be quite significant when it comes to monopolizing use of a word, particularly one coined for a new product or service, because trademarks are more completely protected by law. The task is to define one's place in the market, which can create enormous competitive advantages, without preventing competitors from having access to words that are necessary to the vocabulary.

Trade dress as a concept has taken on significance in recent years. Trade dress refers to an entire image. It has been applied to things as diverse as labels on wine bottles to the uniforms worn by waitresses, together with table settings and the outdoor architecture of Mexican restaurants. The trade dress is the total, unique image of a product or the enterprise providing services. While it may include individual elements that themselves are trademarks (e.g., a bottle of soda may have the mark "Coca Cola," along with the red stripe and a distinctive bottle shape), it is the totality of the elements that makes trade dress. As with other marks, trade dress can be exclusively claimed by its owner.

This fact highlights one of the crucial differences between copyright and trademark law, and underscores the competitive importance of trademarks. Copyrights are granted for limited periods of time and the law is designed to prevent copying. If two people independently create the same work, with minor variations or even none at all, unless there is proven copying by one or the other, each can hold a copyright on their work and use it to the full extent of the law. And while fair use permits certain use without consent, similarity of works, in and of itself, is not dispositive of the legal question of infringement.

Trademarks, by contrast, are monopolies in a word or phrase. The key requirement is "first to use in commerce," and the test for infringement is whether there is a likelihood of confusion between two marks. As a monopolist, a shrewd trademark owner can foreclose competitors from exploiting a word or phrase, and thus gain competitive advantage. When launching new product lines, popular trademarks bring a special lift to a new marketplace entry, even for untested products or services.

In the late 1980s, "USA Today—The Television Show," a newly conceived first-run program produced by Gannett Co. (publisher of *USA Today*) and Grant Tinker, entered the syndicated marketplace with over 170 stations lined up to carry the show. The presales, made without a pilot, were based on the popularity of the newspaper and its alliance with a very successful television producer. Despite the success in establishing affiliations, the show itself failed to measure up to expectations. It floundered while the producers discovered the show was not attracting viewers, and they tried to remake its image. The advantage afforded by the extension of the *USA Today* brand was squandered because the producers were not able to deliver a successful program. Had the show reached its potential, it would have become a powerful demonstration of the persuasive exploitation of trademarks. As matters played out, it illustrated the risks of associating a valuable trademark with an underachieving product.

A similar fate befell Coca Cola when it launched its highly promoted "New Coke" drink, only to discover the public loved the old "Classic Coke" formula. Nevertheless, successful trademarks will always inspire the spin-off. The launch of MSNBC, the cable channel merging Microsoft and NBC, underscores the never-ending search for the effective brand extension. In sum, the proper handling of trademarks, from their inception, can provide lasting benefit to the owner.

Trademark Continuum: Fanciful, Arbitrary, Suggestive, Descriptive, and Generic

Think of trademarks existing on a continuum, like a ruler.

TRADEMARK CONTINUUM

Greater Protection				Less Protection
Fanciful	Arbitrary	Suggestive	Descriptive	Generic
Kodak	Eagle	Discovery	E.R.	Cellular telephone
Polaroid	Sable	Chicago Hope	The Golf Channel	Television
Exxon		Nickelodeon	Family Channel	Radio

At one end, there are *fanciful marks*, terms that have no dictionary meaning. They are coined terms, like Kodak, Polaroid, and Exxon. They are invented and then invested with an image. Based on the success and breadth of the products and services, and their marketing, they become unique identifiers that are granted significant trademark recognition.

Continuing along the ruler, there are *arbitrary marks*, those that contain words or phrases that are commonplace, but that are applied in an uncommon way. There is no dictionary connection of the word *eagle* to potato chips or *sable* to cars. However, the words themselves connote images that the commercial users decide to capitalize on. Choosing an arbitrary word and associating it with a new good or service is not only a creative, but also a complex task. It usually requires substantial effort in marketing and image building. Creating new associations with words that never existed before, or words that have no logical association with one's products or services, is not an easy task. However, when done successfully, the identification of fanciful and arbitrary marks with products or services establishes the most useful and long-lasting bonding of all trademarks.

Most people, even including those creative types in the media, gravitate to familiar words or phrases that they try to use in inventive ways, suggesting what their product or service is about. They seek to exploit words or phrases that already have an association in the consumer's mind and thus create *suggestive marks*. Titles of cable channels and television shows fit this bill routinely: Nickelodeon, Discovery, and "Chicago Hope" are but a few examples of titles that function as media service marks because they are suggestive of their content.

Nickelodeon is a clever illusionary mark, because it conjures up associations with entertainment and children, without explicitly saying "children's channel." Discovery is also an intriguing title because it suggests programming fare that is exploratory, and most likely about science and nature, without expressly stating so. In trademark terms, these titles are invested with greater potential for protection against competitors or others who would try to trade on their reputation. When a video store put children's videos into a section called "Discovery Zone," the network raised some flack. It argued that the use either implied an association with the Discovery Channel or an endorsement. The matter concluded when the video store ended the practice.

The program title, "Chicago Hope," does not tell you much about content, other than you might expect it to be set in the city of Chicago. Its prime time competitor, "ER," uses a title that describes its content more explicitly. There is little question that a show entitled "ER" will have an emergency room theme; by contrast, "Chicago Hope" does not so expressly define what it is about.

In trademark terms, "ER" is a *descriptive mark*. The distinguishing feature of a descriptive mark is that it states the essential elements or the content of the product or service. One way to characterize the distinction is as follows: If you can close your eyes and know what the product or service is about, the mark is descriptive. When one hears "The Family Channel" or "The Golf Channel" in connection with cable services, it requires no leap of faith or mental gymnastics to understand what programs these channels will feature.

The phrase *generic mark* is really a misnomer, because if the word or phrase is generic, it identifies a category of goods or services, rather than a source. *Television, radio,* and *cellular telephone* are generic. They cannot function as trademarks because they are inherently incapable of helping a consumer to distinguish one source from another. Sometimes, a fanciful mark becomes so successful in the marketplace that the public and competitors treat it as generic. That is death to a trademark.

Concern about a fanciful mark turning generic is why Xerox, Inc. has worked so hard over the years informing consumers that "Xerox" is a trademark for photocopy machines. As the ads advise, one does not make a "xerox," one uses a "Xerox photocopy machine," or creates a "Xerox photocopy." Sometimes, this can be a losing battle. At one time, aspirin and cellophane were trademarks. With common usage, they became generic.

This fact underscores the grammar of trademark law. When developing trademarks, think "adjectives." Properly used, trademarks qualify a type of good or service and, in sentences, should serve to modify a noun. Oftentimes, the noun is unclear, but that does not mean it does not exist. "Cheers," that is, the Cheers television show, a suggestive mark for a program about a bar, is also a thriving trademark enterprise. The word and logo are associated with Cheers T-shirts, Cheers mugs, Cheers calendars—you name it. Every kind of product can bear the trademark; however, in all instances, the proper placement of the mark is as that little old adjective.

Strength of a Mark

After the trademark continuum, there is another continuum to understand, which we'll call the protection continuum. This concerns the strength of a mark. Fundamentally, there are strong marks and weak marks. The stronger the mark, the more legal protection it is entitled to receive.

PROTECTION CONTINUUM

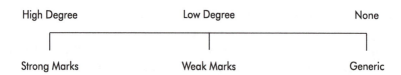

High Degree	Low Degree	None
Strong Marks	Weak Marks	Generic

Marks gain strength in two ways: First, they are conceived with strength, because they are fanciful, arbitrary, or suggestive terms. The more a mark is removed from generic and descriptive terminology, the better its chances to be "strong." Second, a mark can be invested with strength by advertising and promotion. Even a weak, descriptive mark can become so well known to the public and the identifier of a unique source that it is entitled to a high degree of trademark protection.

Cable News Network describes quite nicely what it is about. However, because it was the first and the only cable news network at its inception, because over 10,000 systems serving over 50 million subscribers carry it, and because its prominent news-gathering success has made it a household name, Cable News Network and its acronym CNN are strong trademarks. Had several cable networks specializing in news been launched at the same time, and had each tried to use the phrase that connects them most simply to the viewers, then *cable news network* might not be a strong trademark for anyone. The competitive use of phrases like The Game Channel, Game Network, and Game TV, all for start-up channels, evidences the dilemma CNN would have had with direct competition in its early years.

Unique Identifiers in Specific Lines of Commerce

The most important feature of a trademark is that it stands for a unique source. If it does, the mark is protectable as a monopoly for its owner. If it does not, then it may not be a useful trademark at all. However, while trademark law grants a monopoly, allowing its owner to remove the mark from the commercial vernacular of competitors, it does so only with respect to the particular classes of the goods and services actually associated with the mark. Because there is a finite number of words or phrases, and because consumers have certain expectations about the relationship between marks and services or goods, not all uses are restricted.

Thus, even though no television series could consider calling itself "ER," no hospital in the country could be prevented from using the phrase "ER" because of the television series. Similarly, if a pharmaceutical firm produces an ER line of medicines, it could not be stopped from employing the phrase because there would be little likelihood of confusion in the public's mind that the medicines originated with the television production.

Sometimes, even popular trademark owners carry their case too far. During the early years of the Reagan administration, a proposal to launch a network of "killer satellites" that could target and destroy enemy forces was proposed. The plan was dubbed "Star Wars" because of its futuristic and out-of-this-world theme. As press reports trumpeted the project, the owners of the popular *Star Wars* film trilogy took offense. A trademark dispute arose, with the film company trying to shoot down the government's use of the phrase. The attack failed, a victim of the old "different class of services" defense. A similar issue surfaced during the 1996 presidential race. Trying to echo Nancy Reagan's antidrug theme "Just Say No," Republican Presidential candidate Bob Dole exclaimed, "Just Don't Do It." Well, guess what shoe company, known for the theme "Just Do It" emerged to complain?

In sum, trademark law protects words or phrases in specific lines of commerce. As soon as one moves to an unrelated field of endeavor, that trademark legal protection may *not* travel. Thus, the word *eagle* may be used not only for potato chips by one company, but for a car by a different company, a hand stapler by a third, and a TV production business by a fourth. Each can use the same trademark without violating a trademark right of another because consumers can readily distinguish the sources of the marks. The strength of a mark is vital to this determination, as is the nature of the mark on the trademark continuum. If the NBC network challenged Newark Banking Company (NBC bank), it would lose. Even though it owns one of the most famous trademarks in the nation, the public's familiarity with acronyms is such that the marketplace could accept both titles. By contrast, a strong *and* fanciful mark like Kodak would be in a much better position to prevent other uses, even in unrelated areas. Kodak Bank or Kodak Television Company would find the venerable film company on its back ASAP.

Likelihood of Confusion

These principles lead to the crucial legal test in trademark law: *likelihood of confusion.* The landmark case that explains this principle is *Polaroid Corp. v. Polarad Electronics Corp.,* known as *Polaroid* for short. Since the law grants monopolies in trademarks, and since there are a limited number of available words or phrases to describe goods and services, the *Polaroid* test looks at a variety of elements to determine if the two marks in question are likely to cause confusion as to source in the minds of a relevant consuming public. If there is a likelihood of confusion, usually the first to use a mark will prevail and the second owner will either lose its rights to the mark or find its market severely restricted. If no likely confusion exists, the two marks can coexist.

The elements of likelihood of confusion, explained in the *Polaroid* decision, include:

- The strength of the marks—are the marks fanciful, arbitrary, suggestive, descriptive, or generic?
- The similarity of the marks—how close are they in sight, sound, and meaning?
- The nature of the goods or services—are they sold in the same channel of commerce?
- Bridging the gap—if they are in different channels of commerce, how likely is the first user to bridge the gap?
- The sophistication of the buyers—are they specialists and able to discern small differences in marks that identify different sources?
- Intent of second comer—was the second user aware of the first, and is there any evidence of intentional copying?
- Evidence of actual confusion—is there documentable evidence that someone has been confused already?
- Quality of the defendant's product—is there a potential for negative publicity?

Anytime a trademark of another is used, these issues must be considered. If a second user cannot satisfactorily explain the use under each of these criteria, then the wisest course would be to choose another word or symbol. We take a closer look at this all important issue in Chapter 10.

Secondary Meaning

While a mark that describes the goods or services (such as "60 Minutes," for a one-hour television show), is usually deemed weak and unprotectable, if the mark becomes well-known to the public as originating from a sole source, it can gain status as a protectable trademark. When a mark achieves this status, it is said to have gained *secondary meaning*. Although there is a primary meaning for the word or phrase, its secondary meaning points to a unique source.

Secondary meaning is secured through the expenditure of two precious commodities: time and money. The longer a mark is used by a sole source and the greater the public's awareness of the mark as originating from the source, the more likely it is that secondary meaning will attach. Therefore, a television program about cooking by European master chefs called, ingeniously, "The Master Chefs," can gain secondary meaning by virtue of its being the only such program so titled, by its achieving solid ratings, and by its having significant public exposure, through advertising and other publicity. There are numerous television programs that readily fit this category, from "Star Search" to "Dallas" to "Friends" and "Monday Night Football."

The issue of who is entitled to secondary meaning in a mark can spark debate. When David Letterman switched from NBC Late Night to CBS, the transfer was marked by public wrangling. Among his television signature items, Letterman wanted to continue his "Top 10" on CBS. NBC resisted, claiming the logo was theirs. The legal dispute was a small subplot in the larger issue of his departure, but CBS ultimately relented and came up with a close, albeit slightly different title, the "Late Show's Top 10 List." Certainly, "Top 10" is descriptive, but NBC claimed, for television purposes, that it had achieved secondary meaning. No one else was doing it, and Dave had been using the phrase for the better part of a decade. While the mark was identified with Letterman, because he created it during his employment by NBC, the network used its status as his employer to claim ownership of his work. The addition of the phrase "Late Show," which was CBS's alternative to "Late Night," separated the marks and gave the new network a sufficient trademark claim that the titles were distinguishable.

Use in Commerce and Intent to Use

A defining characteristic of a trademark is that it must be *used*. With one important exception recently crafted by federal law, if a trademark is not used in commerce, no rights attach. Talking about a mark to friends does not create any trademark rights. Sitting at a computer and composing a business plan does not create trademark rights. By contrast, marketing a product or telecommunicating a program creates rights. For many years, the use could have been token. Merely sending a mock-up of a magazine to a colleague in a different state was sufficient to support "use" under the law prior to 1988.

However, since 1988 the use had to be more than token, although by any measure it need not be very extensive. The reason for the change in 1988 was that Congress added the concept of *intent to use*. Henceforth, as soon as one has an idea for a title or mark, one can file a request with the U.S. Patent and Trademark Office (PTO) and effectively reserve the mark. Once the application is approved, it can be held in reserve for up to three years, provided there remains a *bona fide* intent to actually carry out the plans to use the mark in commerce. That generous opportunity has altered the trademark landscape. Now, the race is on to file for a trademark. If one maintains an intention to use, there is every legal right to hold onto a title for three years. That can be a valuable asset against a competitor.

Geographic Coverage of Marks

One of the important limitations on use of trademarks is geography. Unless the user of a trademark has applied with the PTO for federal registration of the mark or intention to use a mark, then the owner of the trademark is entitled to protection only in the geographic area where the mark has actually been used. Typically, trademark protection for nonregistered marks runs on a state-by-state basis. Thus, the same trademark can be owned by someone in Oregon and another person in Massachusetts. In broadcasting, this occurs frequently, for example, when a local radio station develops a format theme (Mix, Cool Jazz, or Hot Hits) and another station in a distant market picks up the same image. Unless protected by federal registration, the phrase can seep out into many markets. While one station may be able to stop a local competitor, a broadcaster or business in a remote region may be free to use its trademark, even if that second party is legally related to the local competitor who was stopped.

These are the core principles of trademark law. But trademarks are regulated by a complex system of federal, state, and common laws. Also, for media aficionados, the Federal Communications Commission (FCC) assigns all sorts of identifiers, such as call signs and telephone numerators, which can have trademark significance. On top of this, there is a fifty-state system of trade name registrations and, with the arrival of the Internet, a government-sponsored system of allocated domain names, the sites that enable you to access remote computers. Let's take a closer look at the trademark systems in the United States.

Chapter 8

The Trademark Systems: Claiming Your Mark

There are three trademark legal systems in the United States: common law, state, and federal. The abiding basis for trademark protection in the United States is "use in commerce." If a word, phrase, or image has been used, then common law rights attach. *Common law* refers to the legal decisions of judges that are based on equity or simple fairness. Therefore, a common law system based on use is our departure point.

Trademark rights are acquired whenever and wherever a mark is adopted and affixed to a good or service that is offered for sale or in relation to commerce. Even if you are unsuccessful in selling the product, trademark rights exist in connection with that good or service. It is the fact that the offer is made that counts. Sometimes, goods are not sold; rather, they are given away. Radio stations and other media outlets will provide promotional items, such as T-shirts, mugs, and hats, at public events to trumpet their changes in formats or new services, such as "WHRX—Miami's HOT ROCK," "KSSS—SEATTLE's STARLIGHT STATION," "WIOF—Wilmington's Island of Fantasies." Not only the call letters, but also the slogans, are trademarks for the operations. Promotional products emblazoned with slogans are designed to identify the station and to fix it as a source in the public's mind. Therefore, the words or symbols are trademarks, and common law protects them as well.

One does not have to "do anything" to acquire common law trademark protection, other than *use the mark*. Once the mark appears in commerce in connection with the good or service, common-law rights attach. In simplest terms, common law rights mean that a degree of exclusivity is secured in the mark. This ensures that neither a local competitor, nor a national enterprise, can later displace a prior trademark owner merely because of local or national regulations. The common-law rights can be used offensively or defensively in the trademark owner's market.

However, since common law rights are local, and since many enterprises want a broader protection for the mark, common law status is often inadequate. For example, when a radio station enters the national advertising or programming markets and seeks to be uniquely identified, common law protection may not cut it. Regional or national protection is a must. Thus, many entities that are concerned with their identifying names and slogans and that spend a significant part of a business budget promoting a mark, need to turn to the state and federal systems of protection.

All states operate a trademark registration system for those who do business in the state. As a practical matter, state registration offers only a few advantages over common law protection. Since common law is usually defined on a state-by-state basis, once a media outlet uses a mark, it is protected in areas where it operates. An FM station in Atlanta has rights throughout the state of Georgia, whether registered with the Secretary of State or not. What are the advantages of state registration?

First, there is notice. The state trademarks are published in a registry, which constitutes effective notice to those doing business in the state. Second, in some localities state registrants are granted certain procedural advantages in the case of disputes, such as a legal presumption that the mark is valid, which helps one meet its legal burdens. Third, experience shows that some judges who rarely deal with trademark disputes are impressed with a state registration. It turns out that the nice paper the registration is printed on can make a difference.

State registrations are inexpensive and quick to obtain. Filing fees vary from $20 to $50 and are often processed in two to four weeks. However, that speed underscores the weakness of the state system. The state registries only look to determine whether an identical mark is already registered and whether the request meets the barest definition of a trademark. There is no assessment as to the appropriateness to register under the standards that assess the legal validity of a mark. As a result, the state registrations are given limited credence by most courts.

By contrast, federal trademark protection is all that a trademark proprietor needs. Once a trademark is registered with the federal government, protection is nationwide. You can go from coast to coast and prevent interlopers from stealing your theme. Whether you care about its being used a thousand miles away is less a point than that federal registrants have the right to stop such uses. Since a core requirement for federal registration is that a mark be used in interstate commerce, and since communication is defined as interstate commerce, all media enterprises can assess their marks and consider them ripe for federal protection.

The federal registration system is staffed by trademark lawyers (examiners) trained in the legal standards. Processing a federal application can take one year or more to complete. With that laborious process, however, comes a host of rights that make federal registration the only system one should consider for important trademarks. Here's why: A federally registered trademark is entitled to

- National protection. As noted, you can defend your rights anywhere in the country, stopping infringers located in distant markets, even those in which you do no business.
- *Prima facie* protectable status. This means that a plaintiff in a trademark dispute can point to the registration as legal proof that the mark is valid and entitled to protection. While courts occasionally reject that conclusion, registration is powerful proof in most lawsuits.
- National notice. The federal records provide constructive notice to the world of the registrant's rights.
- Use of the official registration notice: ®. Only a federally registered mark can be associated with the notification, which places legal burdens on anyone misusing marks with such notice.
- Penalties, including triple damages and attorneys' fees, can be awarded in special cases of infringement.
- International status. Under international trademark treaties, federal applicants are granted special filing status in many foreign countries.
- Domain names on the Internet are afforded unique protection. Under a new system of registering domain names, only federal registrants can be readily assured that third parties do not steal marks.

With all these advantages, what are the steps in securing a federal registration? First, conduct a *search*. Whenever a company identifies a new trademark that it intends to exploit, it is simply foolish not to research its availability. Because developing a trademark means investing time and resources into creating a public connection between the mark and the company, and because once a mark is established it becomes a headache or worse to change, failure to attend to this practical step leaves one vulnerable to forces unknown. In some instances, the dispute can be characterized in Biblical terms—a David and Goliath trademark affair. One such case involved a very large media firm that should have known better. It did not conduct a search when it adopted a new look, but it spent millions on the changeover.

In the mid-70s, NBC tried to uplift its image. The once mighty network had fallen on some rocky times and slipped behind CBS and upstart ABC. NBC hired a Madison Avenue PR firm, which designed a new logo and market-tested it. It concluded NBC should shelve the long-used peacock and N-B-C chimes in favor of a sleek, cool block letter "N." The network announced the shift in closed-door meetings with staff and affiliates and rolled it out with much fanfare on a bright and hopeful New Year's Day amidst football hoopla and huge audiences.

Unbeknownst to NBC, one viewer of that New Year's Day initiation was a station executive at a public television station in Nebraska. That new NBC logo sure looked familiar. Indeed, it was identical to the University of Nebraska's Educational Television Network logo, developed by an art designer for about $30 and in use for over six months. When NBC was warned about the similarity of the marks, the network rebuffed the Nebraska station brusquely. A trademark infringement suit was filed, during which it was learned that NBC *never had conducted a search*. Despite a multimillion dollar budget, not one penny went into researching the availability of the block "N" for broadcasting. Based on its priority of use, Nebraska had the upper hand. NBC soon understood its legal vulnerability and settled the case, sending a fully loaded mobile van with a fortune in equipment to the University. Oh, yes, NBC also paid Nebraska's legal fees. All because someone forgot to conduct a search.

Trademark searching is like digging a hole looking for something that may not exist—a confusingly similar mark in an overlapping area of commerce. How long should one dig? The simplest answer is until you feel comfortable based on the importance of the mark to your business. For most uses, a search of federal and state trademark registries and pertinent databases of newspapers and magazines, corporate name listings, and phone directories should suffice. Trademark specialists and research firms can do the trick for well under $1,000. However, if the mark selected is commonly used and the costs to launch a business are substantial, then more extensive digging is appropriate. When Exxon Company was looking for that right word to replace its collection of Esso, Humble, Standard Oil, and others, it spent tens of thousands of dollars searching and clearing the title. That research was reported to be so extensive it turned up a garage owned by the Exon family of Nebraska, and Exxon bought the name rights.

Second, once the mark is clear, file for federal registration. While state registration will do for strictly local uses, for any mark of importance, only federal registration need be considered. Filing with the Trademark Office [part of the Patent and Trademark Office (PTO or U.S. Trademark Office) within the Department of Commerce] involves preparing a two-page application, paying the filing fee ($245 per mark per class), and attaching some examples of material showing the mark in use (in PTO parlance, "specimens").

If the mark is not in commerce yet, the 1988 Trademark Revision Act allows the filing of an application for an "intent to use" (ITU) mark. This filing allows for the reservation of a trademark that the applicant has a good-faith intent to exploit. One has up to three years after the initial grant to actually start using the mark. The rules require notice to the PTO every six months after the mark is "allowed" to show that plans are still progressing in order to maintain the ITU.

The importance of these federal filings cannot be understated. Once a first user registers a mark, it acquires national protection and has a virtual monopoly on the right to use the mark for its products or services. That monopoly can be enforced in any federal court in the nation. Also, the federal process allows a registrant to apply for protection in other countries under the rules of certain treaties. One scam to be aware of is that some savvy foreigners register popular U.S. trademarks in their own territory and then lie in wait for the U.S. companies to export goods or services into that land. When they do, the foreigners inform the U.S. company that to use their own mark they have to pay a license fee. That threat can be avoided by a trademark owner having the forethought to register trademarks in certain countries as well as the United States. Television and film distributors, in particular, who make much of their income from overseas licensing, must be especially attentive, lest their names and reputations be pilfered by unscrupulous competitors abroad.

Third, be attentive to the *federal trademark family tree*. (See Figure 8.1.) Registration is neither automatic nor immediate. The PTO assigns all applications to an examiner, who scrutinizes the application for proper form and compliance with legal standards.

The most crucial test is to assure that the mark is not confusingly similar to another registered mark. Although the same mark can be used for unrelated goods or services (e.g., KOOL is a radio station's call letters and a brand of cigarettes), if the services or goods are related and the marks closely resemble each other (e.g., KOOL for a radio station and "Kool Jazz" for a radio program), then the PTO can reject the application.

Before denying an application for registration, the PTO issues an "action letter," to which a response is required within six months. The sooner an action letter is answered, the faster the application is processed. Sometimes, answers can be provided in a short phone call. After final action, an application is either approved and published in the *Official Gazette* for "opposition" or denied. If published, there is a thirty-day period in which parties who believe they will be harmed by registration can oppose the registration. (The thirty-day opposition period can be extended for up to ninety more days on request.)

An opposition forces a legal proceeding before the PTO's Trademark Trial and Appeal Board (TTAB). The TTAB conducts a hearing, during which the parties engage in discovery, much like in formal court cases. Discovery includes the process of asking for written answers to questions (interrogatories) and taking oral testimony from witnesses under oath (depositions). The TTAB has a second stage or testimony period, during which each side files the key information it intends to rely on for its arguments. Briefs are filed and the TTAB rules on the opposition.

If registration is denied by the examiner, the applicant can give up the quest or file an appeal with the TTAB. If an appeal is taken, the TTAB either agrees with the examiner and denies the application, or permits it to be published for opposition.

In any instance in which a litigant is unhappy with the TTAB's final decision, an appeal process is available. In cases of opposition, the losing party can head to the U.S. Court of Appeals for the Federal Circuit. In application cases, the rejected applicant can appeal to the Federal Circuit or file an action in federal district court, literally starting the process all over again.

The last resort after the Federal Circuit is the U.S. Supreme Court. It is very, very, very unlikely that any appeal to the U.S. Supreme Court would be heard, much less successful. Trademark rulings by the highest court come once every few years.

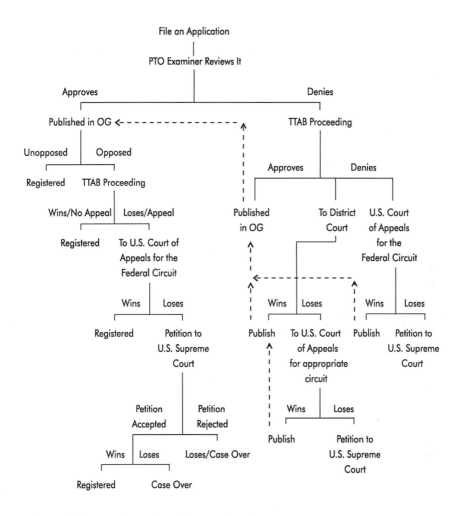

Figure 8.1 Trademark application family tree

If the applicant is successful in obtaining a registration, there is still a potential catch. The trademark law allows a challenge to a registration within the first five years after registration. In particular, a prior user can ask the PTO to cancel the registered mark. A cancellation proceeding is much like an opposition and is handled by the TTAB as well. After the fifth year of registration passes, a registered mark becomes "incontestable." While this does not mean there is no basis whatsoever to challenge a mark—if a mark was obtained fraudulently or if it becomes generic, it can always be questioned—for all intents and purposes, it is hard to overcome an incontestable mark.

Another important thing to understand about the federal trademark registration process is that there are *two registries*. The Principal Register is the place where all protectable marks end up. There is also a backup registry, called the Supplemental Register. Trademarks that examiners believe are descriptive, but not generic, can be enrolled in the latter.

While the Supplemental Register has a "second-class citizen" feel about it—descriptive marks cannot succeed in many claims of infringement or confusion—there are two good reasons to consider it as an alternative to simply abandoning the quest for registration. If a mark is registered there for five years, its owner can petition to move it to the Principal Register and claim full trademark rights. It's a way of establishing secondary meaning by longevity. A Supplemental Register mark will also be used by an examiner as a basis to reject someone else's application. Together these are sufficient reasons to view the Supplemental Register kindly if it is just not possible to secure registration on the Principal Register.

Fourth, don't forget to *maintain* and *renew* the registration. Trademarks are registered for terms of ten years; however, during the first term of registration, the owner of a trademark is required to file an affidavit of continued use in the fifth year after registration to maintain it. Once the affidavit attesting to the fact that the mark is still in business for the applicant is filed, the mark is deemed "incontestable," and kept on the registry for the full term.

After ten years, all trademarks must be renewed by the filing of a renewal application. The ten-year rule took effect in 1988; previously, registrations were granted for twenty years. As legal reform, the Congress sought to clean up "deadwood," marks that stayed registered long after the owner discontinued use. In the media, with themes changing quickly, registered marks may lose vitality after a few years. Nevertheless, the registrations give the owner leverage over later users of the same mark.

There are two other parts to the media mark system that deserve mention. First, for all radio and television stations, the Federal Communications Commission (FCC) is the "call letters" gatekeeper. Whenever a new station is licensed or an existing station wants to change its formal name, the FCC must approve the choice of call letters. Up until about fifteen years ago, the FCC acted like a mini-PTO and heard complaints by competitors who believed a call letter assignment was too similar to another assignment in the market. Thus, radio station KLUB could challenge KLUG from being assigned to a station in its market.

As competition over call letters became more intense, the FCC abandoned its mediator role. It adopted a rule that encouraged stations with a dispute to work the matter out privately or to go to court. As long as the letters were available, they could be assigned. But like any other trademark, the call letters could be challenged by a party claiming likelihood of confusion. Another change implemented over the last decade coincided with the FCC's breakdown of some of the ownership limitations. The rules were relaxed enough to allow unrelated radio and television stations to share common letters. WRAD-FM and WRAD-TV no longer had to belong to the same owner. While FCC assignment rules allowed this to work, if WRAD-FM objected, trademark principles could be called on to prevent the assignment of WRAD-TV to an unrelated owner.

In Chapter 24, we'll have a lot to say about trademarks and the Internet. For the present time, keep a note that issues of trademark use and misuse are cropping up in cyberspace, and federally registered trademarks are granted special protection when it comes to the assignment of domain names (the key terms in Internet addresses).

That's the trademark system. Now let's move on to the acquisition of trademarks.

Chapter 9

Strategy for Acquiring Trademark Rights: A "How To" for Branding

Trademark law has the goal of protecting two interests: one, the investment of those in business, who create words or symbols to identify a source; the other, the consumers, who rely on a mark as a symbol of quality and an association with a known source. Unlike copyright law, which only secures protection against copying, trademark law grants a *monopoly* to use a word or symbol in commerce. In other words, under trademark law even if the second user does not know of the original use, it may be forced to stop an infringing use.

As we have already noted, but it bears repeating, *the nature of the rights one secures in a trademark will depend on a number of factors.* Sometimes, planning and forethought can result in a master strategy for identifying and securing trademark rights. Other times, the acquisition is accidental, the success of symbols in the market that might not have been anticipated. Because the second case is common, it is useful to do a periodic inventory of the key words and symbols actually used, and to determine which, if any, are really important assets for the business. The most important should be protected by federal registration. Those of lesser importance could be protected by state registration. To make this determination, consider "The Five Hows":

1. How distinctive is the mark?
2. How much investment has the owner made in the mark?
3. How well is the mark known to consumers?

4. How diverse are the goods or services offered by the owner?
5. How likely is it that another's trademark use will confuse the public as to source?

As you answer these questions, it will become clear which marks are important to your operations. With that essential determination in hand, a strategy for ensuring protection for the mark will then develop.

1. How distinctive? In the media, some phrases endure and others disappear. The CBS "eye" is of immense value to the network. It is a suggestive mark made strong by unique usage that indelibly stamps a program's source. When CBS finally chose to enter the cable market, it developed an "Eye on People" logo and look. By contrast, many radio stations have developed descriptive, weak trademark themes for their formats, such as "Beautiful 98" for an easy listening station on FM 98.3. On the trademark continuum, this title is doubly descriptive: "Beautiful" describes its music and "98" is its geographic address on the dial. Given the radio allocation assignment rules, the "Beautiful 98" format may be repeated in many broadcast markets. Therefore, stations should be cautious when they invest primary identity in phrases of limited trademark distinctiveness.

2. How much investment? Take a look at expenditures over time. Promotional advertising is often a hefty chunk of any operation's budget. The more money invested in repeating thematic images to the public, the more important those images are. Trademarks are at the core of the imagery. With our "Beautiful 98" example, a station may find that between billboards, on-air identification (often as many as twenty times per hour, every hour, every day), and television or print advertising, the investment in a phrase can be substantial. This underscores a truism of trademark law. *Every business has a name and an identity.* Make sure that the ways you are known to the public justify the expenditures you will have to make to compete. The more distinctive a mark, from a trademark law perspective, the better. Be inventive and clever. Remember the trademark continuum: The more fanciful or arbitrary the mark, the stronger the protection.

3. How much consumer awareness? Heavily promoted marks will be known to consumers. Also, events can make marks more popular. It is often surprising that while stations may be forced by circumstances to relinquish a mark, the consumer may keep an asso-

ciation with well-known firms for many years. Call letters are a prime example. When stations change hands, alter formats, and change call signs, the public can be slow to adjust to the change. It is not surprising that years after a format and call letter switch, many consumers still remember the former call sign.

This fact of consumer awareness can create an advantage for a cagey competitor who picks up abandoned call letters. If diary-keepers, the sturdy souls paid to track viewing or listening habits, and thus make ratings possible, retain a former station's call sign in their minds, they may award credit to the wrong station. However, if a federal trademark registration was secured for the call sign, the former owners could stymie a competitor's plan and prevent use of the call letters in the home market.

4. How diverse are the products? Brand extension is often a fundamental strategy. We start with the understanding that some trademarks are *the signature* for a company; for example, Disney's rendition of Mickey's ears is world renowned. If one sees this symbol on *any product or service*, the connection in the public's mind is instantaneous. Disney owns that image in the marketplace. Not only can it stop others from developing confusion to the detriment of the public or the company, but it can also leverage the mark to extend into new markets and diversify. When Disney launched a cable channel and when it opened a chain of stores, the logo for the company was right there. Disney attached the mark to a variety of goods, thereby diversifying the mark's role in commerce.

5. How likely is it that another's mark will create confusion? As we have often repeated, the key issue in trademark law is the likelihood of confusion as to source. When a strong trademark is used in connection with certain goods or services, it can be said to have a "penumbra effect," a halo around it that translates into an association with other goods or services. Even if a trademark owner does not sell certain goods or offer certain services, the public may assume it does. Kodak does not own movie theaters, but if one theater chain opened with that name, the film manufacturer could object. How likely it is that consumers will be confused, even in the absence of direct competition, is a pertinent issue.

There is also an important interrelationship among copyrights, trademarks, and competition. Many important copyrights can be protected as trademarks as well. Cartoon characters, such as Mickey Mouse, fit this mold. Originally conceived as a drawing, that is, a copyrighted work, the mouse has become the symbol of the Disney empire. Long after the copyrights in the original films are in the public domain, Disney will prevent third party misuse of its works by trademark protection. Even though the original animated works will be freely available for recirculation by anyone in the public, no one will be able to commercialize Mickey without Disney's approval. And the same can be said for Minnie, Donald Duck, Daisy, Goofy, Snow White, and all the animated folks. While the storylines may be free to develop, the names, animation, appearance, even voices of the Disney characters will be protected as trademarks of the company.

Answering "The Five Hows" leads to a crucial practice of trademark law for the twentieth century: branding. When a mark is important, claim it and let the world know it stands for you as the source. Even if the public does not "really know" who "Westinghouse," or "General Electric," or "Intuit" is, the constant and aggressive use of branding establishes trademark imagery in the public's mind.

Here are the key hints for branding:

Do that search at the very first opportunity! If there is going to be any significant financial investment in a mark, start out with a search. The wisdom of clearing titles early is proven by the bitter disappointment of many who learn well after the fact that third party use of the same mark is an insurmountable barrier to plans. In some cases, if the early search discloses a prior use, the first user may be willing to sell its rights, and to do so for a lot less than after a trademark is launched. If you doubt this, just compare Exxon's handling of the Exon name with the NBC–Nebraska "N" logo dispute.

If the mark is clear and you think it will be useful, *register it.* Once cleared, if the mark is important, register it with the PTO. If the plans do not call for initiation of the goods or services for a period of time (more than a few months), file an ITU. The filing establishes rights fixed by law, and the modest fees associated with the effort will repay themselves over and over again during the ensuing years.

Brand all uses of the mark. Until a mark is registered, one should not use the federal registration notice ®, but by all means use "TM" or "SM" anytime you can. These layman's symbols for trademarks and service marks put the public on notice and bring instant recognition that a trademark is afoot.

Be alert to third party mischief. Keep a watchful eye in your immediate marketplace and elsewhere for third party uses that create confusion. Remember, copying can be a sign of flattery, but each unauthorized use that continues unimpeded in the marketplace dilutes the distinctiveness of a mark and can lead to a loss of rights.

Take action when necessary. Failure to stop known third-party infringements can result in the loss of rights vis-à-vis that entity and may, over time, seriously diminish all trademark rights. The law gives a monopoly to aid in the orderly working of the marketplace for the consumer and the business. If the business fails to protect its interest, the consumer may come to rely less on the marks as a sign of unique source identification. At that point, any trademark rights that might have been claimed could be lost forever.

Chapter 10

Likelihood of Confusion:
The Acid Test

Protection of trademarks has a very concrete meaning. Under federal law, common law, and state statutes, a trademark owner can prohibit the use of the same or a confusingly similar mark. Injunctive relief can be secured to order the cessation of use and the destruction of offending merchandise. The trademark owner is also allowed to trace profits of the infringer and to obtain lost revenues. Sometimes, the monetary elements are hard to determine; however, if a sale has been made by the infringer or the trademark owner's ongoing business has suffered a decline in funds, then the connection is arguably there. It would be up to the infringer to justify that the relationship to gain and loss does not exist. The more egregious the trademark theft, the less likely the court will be willing to hear the rationale.

As copyright law sanctions certain uses as "fair use," trademark law also has a corollary. The key concept is analogous, although not expressly set forth in statutory language. Take *Twister*, for example. While Universal Pictures may register the word as a trademark for its popular film and spin-off video game, action figures, and theme park, the storyline of weather chasers does not belong exclusively to anyone. Would a film called *Tornado!* or a theme park ride named *Hurricane!* infringe on the trademark rights of Universal? Could a television station launch a series of news inserts called *Twister,* along with its own images and thematic music?

The answer lies in trademark analysis. The questions to which we always return bear on the likelihood of confusion: Is there likely to be confusion as to the source? Would a consumer be confused into thinking the origin of the program or the theme ride is the same as the familiar title? Proving confusion is fundamental to establishing trademark rights. Whenever a trademark analysis arises, these are the questions to ask:

1. *Are the words or symbols used identical?*
If they are, the most crucial part of the case is established. However, even identical words do not make a claim of trademark infringement a certain winner. For example, *Twister* for a movie and Twister for a toilet bowl cleaner share the identical word. Nevertheless, since the word has dictionary meaning, it starts out as "weak." For the toilet bowl cleaner, the notion of "twister" has suggestive qualities. How strong is the association of the words to the products? How much advertising or publicity has developed around the word to associate it with a source is a key factual question. And remember, there are judgment calls going on in assessing the likelihood of confusion.

A few years ago, courts did flip-flops on the question of whether the phrase, "Here's Johnny," so well identified with "Tonight" host, Johnny Carson, was infringed by a toilet bowl cleaner called "Here's Johnny." Carson lost in district court but won on appeal, establishing the important principle—don't mess with Johnny.

2. *If not identical, how close are the words in sound and meaning?*
If they are not identical, but have some differences, then the analysis becomes trickier. For example, let's assume the movie *Twister* spawns its own enterprises, including a syndicated television series and merchandise, such as lunch boxes, notepads, T-shirts, and soft drinks. All of these uses, on products and services, can be registered as trademarks for the movie studio. Now, let's also assume that some competitors want to tap into *Twister* mania, and they start an enterprise, called Tornado. The two marks are distinguishable both aurally and visually. However, their meanings are virtually identical. If the competing project was dubbed Hurricane, it would be a few steps removed. For trademark confusion purposes, the chances of the public being confused and thinking that the source of *Twister* and Tornado was the same would be reasonably high, but less so for Hurricane because the word means something else and does not begin with the letter "T." Nevertheless, the fact that the words do not share similar meanings is not, in and of itself, the only consideration.

3. *How similar are the goods or services?*

In the Twister-Tornado example, we are positing the same goods or services—TV shows or films and spin-off merchandise. In the case of Johnny Carson, the products were very dissimilar—a TV personality and a toilet-bowl scrub brush. The closer the products or services and their lines of commerce, the more likely the public is to be confused about source. Even if the products are dissimilar, a reasonable consumer expectation that the different product line could originate from the complaining party helps the first user. Since so many media products create new lines of business, market perception can be very fluid. Whether a long distance phone company such as MCI sells branded telephones or not, consumers would assume it does. However, a consumer would scratch his head if he saw an MCI brand of coffee. Confusion? Well, maybe, but maybe not.

4. *Are the marks strong or weak?*

If the mark in question is *fanciful* or *arbitrary*, and if it rates high on the strength meter, then there is a greater likelihood that, even with dissimilar products, confusion will be found. Strength can be a vital factor in reaching a favorable conclusion for a first user.

5. *What is the intent of the second comer?*

In some instances of confusion, a problem materializes accidentally. The parties do not know each other and the crossing of paths in commerce is unplanned. Certainly, NBC did not deliberately try to rough up the University of Nebraska when it adopted the block "N" logo. However, in the case of "Here's Johnny," the fame of Mr. Carson was known, and the toilet bowl company wanted to be cute and play off of the familiar phrase. While parody is respected in copyright, its role in trademark law is more complicated. Because controlling market image is crucial to effective use of trademarks, the law is less tolerant when a commercial use is made of a famous phrase or mark, even if the intent is parody. Knowledge of the original use, and a plan to copy it, can be one of the decisive factors in a finding of trademark infringement.

6. *Is there any evidence of actual confusion?*

Actual confusion is easy to measure. Have there been any misdirected phone calls or letters? Did someone pay a bill from company A by sending it to company B instead? In a radio slogan dispute, a small town station showed evidence that local merchants had complained that the station was going to raise advertising rates to support a big media blitz. It turned out that the expensive promotional campaign was for a larger market station, whose service area overlapped the small town. Even though the small station was on the periphery of the large station's market, proof of actual confusion was persuasive on the issue of likelihood of confusion.

Despite this result, a basic but ironic tenet of trademark law is that actual confusion is only evidence of likelihood of confusion, not conclusive proof that it exists. Why? Because even though some folks may be confused, that does not mean that marks are likely to confuse *reasonable* consumers. It's a variation on the old saying about fooling some of the people some of the time.

7. Are the consumers sophisticated?

Defining the market for the goods or services, and knowing the level of sophistication of the customers, are important facts in trademark disputes. In many media disputes, the consumers are professionals who, it can be argued, can readily distinguish between sources of services or products. For example, television station engineers are the consumers for a station's technical equipment. While Jerrold is a known and respected brand of various electronic devices, would a new equipment manufacturer, Jerry, create confusion among these seasoned engineers? Probably not; however, if the products made their way into the mass marketplace, and ordinary consumers were purchasing them, the conclusion might be different.

8. What about the quality of the goods or services?

The facts would raise additional sympathy for the first trademark owner if the quality of the second product was clearly inferior. In that case, even sophisticated consumers might be negatively inclined to the first user based on the fear that the products were related and the respected name failed to maintain acceptable standards.

9. Is there any survey evidence?

More and more, courts want to see some survey research when it comes to proving the likelihood of confusion. Especially if the case does not involve identical marks in similar product or service lines, polling a responsible sample to support the claim of confusion is good form in trademark disputes.

Survey research, which can be discovered by opposing parties in litigation, must be handled very carefully. The wrong results can doom a case more quickly than anything else, so it is important for the research to be done carefully, sometimes in stages. A small telephone sample of twenty-five to fifty consumers can help refine the research and confirm instincts. If the results suggest that confusion is likely, then a larger sample in the 200 range should be conducted. Professional firms that are experienced in surveying should be consulted from the outset, and they should be asked to serve as witnesses in the event of a trial.

But any trademark litigant should be forewarned that survey results can be surprising. Such was the case for an easy listening station, located on 98.9 FM, called Easy 99. After experiencing three poor ratings books in a row, the station changed formats to MOR and shifted its logo to MIX98. Seeing an opening, a competing station on 99.9 FM (Oldies), whose oldies format performed poorly, changed its name to the zippier Z99.

Fireworks erupted when the easy listening station discovered that ratings diary-keepers, inattentive to the logo change, were writing in 99 FM and Arbitron was crediting all the entries to Z99. In a trademark infringement action, the easy listener claimed "99" as its mark and did a survey. The results were "mixed" to say the least. While some survey participants correctly identified "99" with our friends at 98.9 FM, others considered it generic for any radio and referenced any of half a dozen different stations, including Oldies 100, Peach 104, and Q93. Making sense of the survey nonsense required a seasoned pro.

Chapter 11

Trademarks and Licensing: The Extra Opportunity

Reputation Counts

Trademark licensing is often spelled with dollar signs. That is because licensing is big business. Whether it is transferring logos to merchandise or granting franchise rights to third parties who will make a business by using a popular mark, well-managed trademarks can generate substantial revenue. Due to the media's broad public exposure, licensing can be a vital source of supplemental revenue for all media outlets. Most enterprises take advantage of the opportunity to circulate T-shirts and coffee mugs. Visit any network, major television station, or movie studio, and there is a company store selling to the public what the staff wears—logo emblazoned clothing.

But trademark licensing goes well beyond that, and for those who are savvy, it offers ways to expand a brand's reputation. Take, for example, the extension of cable channels such as Discovery and ESPN. Not only have these networks created clearly defined programming niches for loyal audiences, but also they have been able to sell video-cassettes and other merchandise branded with their logos. Whether they created the product, acquired someone else's works, or gave another manufacturer a license to use their logo, placing their trademarks on the tapes ups the price the market will bear for the works. Similarly, when Discovery bought The Nature Stores in 1996, it did so with the realization that selling nature-oriented products was a "natural," and that the most practical way to achieve brand extension was to move into the retail market. For PBS, the public television network, licensing is viewed as a potential supplement that can cushion drastic cuts in federal funding.

Characters are also important elements in media trademarks. As noted, Mickey Mouse is a Disney franchise; ET a symbol for Universal and its creator, Steven Spielberg. Today, nary a theatrical motion picture is made without consideration of the vast potential of character licensing and extension of the mark to unrelated goods or services, but related revenue streams.

For example, virtually every children's film coming out of Hollywood has mandatory associations with fast-food chains; products, such as dolls, action figures, lunch boxes, and notepads; and amusement park thrill rides. The extension of the copyrighted work into products developed by a theme or character is essential to justifying the unimaginable costs of creation and marketing of major motion pictures and other big-time media programs. Even as film editing of *Jurassic Park*, *The Lion King*, and *Twister* were being completed, plans for exploiting catalogues of merchandise were well underway. It has become *de rigueur* for children's films to hook up with a fast-food franchise, such as McDonalds, Burger King, or Taco Bell.

When planning trademark licensing, whether as a licensee or licenser, there are a number of key things to keep in mind:

1. Register as a federal trademark. If a mark is going to be a centerpiece in licensing, it should be registered with the U.S. Trademark Office. Registered marks are entitled to the strongest legal protection. Registered owners and authorized licensees can use the official registration notice, ®, which provides not just public notice but can offer help in marketing.

2. Cover all necessary uses. Ensuring that the anticipated uses match with the program is vital. It is always easiest to deal with licensing matters up front. If the program is underway and uses that are needed are not covered by the license, there can be confusion, lost opportunities, even legal liability. Pay attention to all possible ways in which the marks are needed or useful for the program you are undertaking.

3. Ensure quality control. The most essential element of a properly devised trademark licensing program is quality assurance. It is the duty of the licenser to be satisfied that the way the mark is used is compatible with its standards. Every agreement should spell out with some precision what constitutes acceptable standards, both with

respect to the products being licensed and the way the mark appears on the goods or in advertising or related uses for services. It may be desirable to preapprove certain samples or to indicate in the understanding that use in a recognized fashion meets the standards of the licenser. The easiest way to *lose a valuable trademark* is to license without quality inspection. Quality control is the *sine qua non* of trademark licensing principles.

4. Make sure it's written down. More confusion reigns when licensing agreements are not in writing. It does not have to be a legal treatise, but there should be a written understanding covering the vital elements of the licensing, including:

- a definition of the mark or marks covered by the agreement
- the term of the license
- quality control
- licensee fees
- termination procedures
- monitoring the marketplace
- what happens after the end of the license

Licensing can take on a life of its own. Effective exploitation of trademark rights can be a lucrative supplement to media revenues and should be part of every business plan. Whether the plan is ultimately successful will depend on some unpredictable factors and some hard work. But don't lose the licensing opportunity.

Chapter 12

Unfair Competition, Publicity, and Privacy: Filling in the Holes

We have just been through a tutorial on trademarks and copyrights. However, as Paul Harvey teases, "and now the *rest* of the story." Copyrights and trademarks are the core issues in content. However, you cannot overlook an important legal triad: unfair competition, privacy, and publicity.

The Rules of Unfair Competition

Buried in the Trademark Law is a real surprise. A special provision of the Lanham Act, Section 43(a), is characterized in simple terms as a *national unfair competition law*. Section 43(a), as it is known, provides that any misrepresentation in commerce is actionable by someone who is "aggrieved." That person can be a consumer or a competitor. It covers not only active misrepresentations, but also false designations of origin, misuse of names, and trademarks. In fact, this rule functions as the national trademark law for unregistered marks.

Little appreciated when it was first passed in 1946, it now is a standard marker in most lawsuits involving trademarks, copyrights, competition, and consumer fraud. Its principles play out in several ways.

When most of the baby boomers were growing up in the fifties and sixties, the rule of thumb was: Don't mention a competitor's brand by name. Comparisons were always between the one household term and "Brand X." Then, in the early seventies, sparked by some lawsuits and the impact of Federal Trade Commission (FTC) rulings, the notion of referring to a competitor's actual mark was encouraged, as long as the representations were truthful. To back up the potential problem of misrepresentations, Section 43(a) became a touchstone for protection.

In the media, advertising sparked the initial debates. Comparing one's product with a leading competitor—everything from soap to autos—meant representing one's goods in relation to another's. Whether the statements were inflated and permissive puffery, or deliberate fraud, Section 43(a) could be called into play to help mediate. For media outlets, there is expanded exposure. As the publisher of potential misrepresentations, radio, television, print, and other outlets are required to be satisfied that the hype is not fantasy. Although an "innocent publisher" clause can be invoked to reduce the sting of false claims, good media practice means knowing what is on your station and being satisfied that extreme claims that identify competitors have a credible rationale.

Section 43(a) is also a sword in the competitive battles in any marketplace. If a material false statement is made in connection with a promotion, or if an unregistered trademark is used by a competitor, this provision opens the door to the federal courts.

For example, when Stephen King complained that his name was used in promotion and on screen for the film, *The Lawnmower Man*, he sought action. Even though he sold film rights to his early storyline, the movie as produced bore no relationship whatsoever to his plot. The only element in common was the title and the use of Stephen King's name. He sued, successfully, to have his name stripped from the title, and all videocassettes had to be reworked to replace his name in the title. All thanks to Section 43(a).

The rule is also employed whenever one's name, voice, image, or likeness is taken without consent. Celebrities as diverse as Woody Allen and Jackie Kennedy Onassis have used this provision to prevent look-alikes from mimicking them in advertisements, thereby confusing the public as to endorsement of a product. Tom Waits and Bette Midler have protected their distinctive voices against commercial imitation and any attempt to imply that Casper the Friendly Ghost is mean to kids could spark an action.

But be warned: Not every use of a name or image will be a violation. If the use is a parody, it may be upheld. When Ginger Rogers sued to stop a movie from being called *Ginger and Fred*, the court reasoned that there was no impression that the legendary actress was endorsing the film. It was a fair and artistic use of the names to create an image essential to the story of the film.

What makes the provision special is its breadth. It relies on the notion that merely presenting a false statement about another in commerce can create a claim by anyone who believes he or she is harmed.

For example, Consumers Union, publisher of *Consumer Reports*, the monthly magazine which prides itself on *unbiased* reporting about products, sued under Section 43(a) when an advertiser, Regina Vacuums, used television commercials to tell the world how well *Consumer Reports* rated its product. From the magazine's perspective, the ad *falsely* implied it endorsed the product. That could have unfairly damaged its reputation for unbiased reporting. Thus, Section 43(a) protects entities who are hurt when the public is misled. In the hands of clever antagonists, the provision is a powerful weapon.

In 1989, Congress clarified the rule to protect "innocent" publishers of false advertisements. Since it is virtually impossible to check every claim in every ad, the rule exempts the media from liability for false advertising that they did not know was false.

Publicity Protection for the Famous

As if Section 43(a) were not enough to think about, there is a whole body of rules enabling famous people to receive money for use of their names and images. Anyone who is a celebrity or who has commercially exploited his or her name, voice, or likeness during life may lay claim to this protection. Generally, the rules of publicity are set forth in state statutes. Sometimes they are found in judges' decisions of fairness or equity. This means consulting with the specific rules of the states where you are doing business to confirm what obligations are afoot.

However, for development of media content with a national reach, you must adopt an approach that respects the most restrictive rules. These will usually be in states such as California and New York. In general, these are the key points to bear in mind:

Nature of the use. Is it commercial? Is there any public interest element, such as news reporting or commentary? Would it qualify for fair use under copyright law? The more you can assert a public interest in the content and the less commercial the status, the better the opportunity to use the image or name.

Who is involved? Is the person famous? Is he or she recognizable by voice, image, likeness, or rendering? Is the person alive or dead? Is the person a minor? The rules help the famous keep what's theirs—commercial exploitation of their persona. If the person is recognizable in any fashion, the rules may apply. Even if the person is dead, there may be rights in the heirs. Elvis Presley's estate is one of the biggest licensors of images. Watch out especially for minors; unauthorized use of their image can be double trouble.

In short, even though a copyrighted work may be in the public domain and free to use by that set of rules, and even though there may be no recognized trademark, either registered or not, the rules of publicity can come into play. The harm from misusing this right can be costly: You may have to pay a penalty, lose a profit, or destroy an infringing product.

And even if the person involved is *not famous*, there may be another headache.

Right of Privacy for the Less Than Famous

Privacy rights is the other side of the coin. Most people have a legal entitlement to anonymity. State rules and common laws protect ordinary folks from

- intrusion into their private affairs
- public disclosure of embarrassing facts
- publicly being placed in a false light
- misappropriation of a name or likeness

For the media, these rules create some bright yellow lights. With mini-cams capturing images right and left, private people are finding their private lives become public. Unlike paparazzi's pictures of royalty, photographs of unknowns should be carefully reviewed before publication. Clearances may be needed unless there is a rationale that supports a public purpose. Since talk is cheap and it is common for guests on radio or television to rant and rave about all sorts of things, and most especially the private lives of unknown people, a wise producer gets a release from every guest and has a ready finger on the "kill button" when in doubt. The releases should not only cover the right to use the images of the guests but should also place the responsibility for the accuracy of the statements that are aired on the guests. There is no 100 percent guarantee against a privacy violation, but the release gives you a firm footing on which to press your case.

Well, there you have it—an overview of copyright and trademark law, and a few distant cousins. Our foundation. Now let's proceed and take a closer look at the uses of these principles in the media, film, and cyberspace.

Part Three

Content: Broadcasting and Film

Chapter 13

News Programming: Competition for Content

Perhaps the most competitive arena in television programming is news and information. During the past decade, there has been a gradual movement of time allocation on television stations from entertainment to news and talk. Just by comparing the schedules of the 1970s with those of the 1990s, one sees the entry of early fringe local newscasts and late night competition. Independent and Fox affiliate stations claim a jump on information over their network affiliate competition with the 10:00 p.m. newscasts. Programs such as "Nightline," "Dateline," "60 Minutes," "Prime Time Live," "20/20," and "48 Hours," presenting up-to-the-minute information, compete for viewership. Paralleling this trend is the evolution of all-news channels on cable television—CNN, MSNBC, Fox News, CNBC, and local 24-hour cable news channels.

Underpinning the development of news programming is the critical issue of content. However, a blurry line marks what you can take from the competition in developing a story and who can claim ownership over the rights to information. Remember the copyright maxim: *Expression is protectable, not ideas.* This is the single most important copyright precept in the development of news programming. Once a story is out, anyone can cover it. You may be able to use portions of another's news programming, even without permission, within the limits of fair use. Since fair use is a fact-based analysis, and since there is much in play when fair use is being assessed, caution must be exercised when using programming developed by the competition.

Moreover, there is a special communications law requirement that interplays with copyright and that affects only television and radio licensees. Under Section 325(a) of the Communications Act, a broadcaster cannot rebroadcast the programming of another station without permission. To some degree, that rule is in conflict with the fair use provision of the Copyright Act, which would allow, even without permission, the use of portions of a third party's programming.

Recall the events involving the gunman who marched into a television station, taking it over, only to kill himself on air. Reporting that compelling story involved use of off-air recordings of another station. Even if the local television competitors successfully developed a fair use claim under copyright law, the Communications Act has no equivalent exemption. Ironically, if the competing news organization using the TV footage was a *cable* news channel, it would have been freer to grab the fair use portion and replay it on the air; however, a local television affiliate in the same market, creating the same story, could be violating a cardinal tenet of its broadcast license. This statutory conflict has never been resolved by the FCC or the courts. Thus, broadcast affiliates need to seek permission if they intend to rebroadcast another station's programming. Fair use may be a defense to a copyright claim, but not to a complaint filed with the FCC.

It is commonplace to have reporters from various media outlets set up outside a locale where news is breaking. Where each is writing his own story, filming events as they unfold, putting his own spin on developments, that is fine. If one station's cameras capture an event unfolding before anyone else, it is a sure bet that, absent the most extraordinary circumstances, fair use will not justify another station's taking the video without permission. So competitive is the marketplace for news, so expensive the process of news gathering, that establishing a fair use to use another's work product is difficult indeed.

Moreover, licensing news and information is an alternative. Because over twenty-five percent of a television station's budget can be allocated to news gathering, recouping some of that investment by licensing third parties, especially those outside the market, is a practical necessity. Wholesaling video stories to organizations such as CNN allows stations to recoup part of their investment, with their news content airing in distant markets.

However, stations have to be careful that they hold the rights they grant to others. There are some misconceptions in this regard. Let's highlight a few:

1. Interviews. Anyone who is interviewed owns his or her own words. While the station can claim copyright to the tape by virtue of direction, camera work, and editing, the subject of an interview holds rights to what he or she says. As a matter of good business practice, it makes sense to obtain releases from anyone who appears on camera. But that is not always practical, since interviews may be in response to fast-breaking events. The use and reuse of the interview can be justified on the basis of implicit consent and fair use. However, if challenged, a station could find that after the initial broadcast, any use, including the licensing of a story to other news outlets, can create a legal exposure. The bottom line is: Don't assume all interview footage shot by a station may be replayed without new permission.

2. Stringers. Many news stories are compiled by news-gathering specialists, who are not regular employees. They may be hired to help produce a specific story or may be in the business of selling stories they develop. In either case, very careful consideration of their contractual relationships is necessary. For example, if a cameraman, who is not a regular employee, is paid to cover a story for an evening newscast and he captures the photo of the year, what uses may the station make of that footage? Unless ownership of the work is transferred to the station, the stringer owns the copyright. One-time broadcast rights are clearly envisioned by the relationship, but how about resale of the footage to other stations or other news media, such as cable channels and foreign stations? How about clipping a photo out of the video and licensing rights to a newspaper or chain of newspapers? What about incorporating the footage into a videocassette on the "news stories of the year?" Absent an agreement, each of the uses constitutes a copyright exploitation that is not owned by the station. Unless a written agreement with the stringer defines his or her contribution as a "work made for hire" or specifically embraces reuses and resale to other media, those rights may not be held by the media. Only if the commonly accepted practices of the industries are very clearly known to cover these uses, or if the station's prior experiences with the stringer make it apparent that both parties anticipated such uses when the employment understanding was made and the fee paid, would the rights be held by the station.

A seminal lawsuit in this area, which awaits resolution as of this writing, involves stringers to newspapers, who are claiming that op-ed articles, which appeared in the daily print edition of newspapers, cannot be used "on-line" without further compensation. The contentions are that the writer owns the copyright and granted the newspaper only the right to first publication. Publishing the text in digital form, through on-line services such as Dialog and Nexus, is an exclusive copyright of the writer, not the newspaper.

Whether the contracts with the stringers cover the issue is the center of the dispute. The news media claim they do. They are also asserting that under copyright law, because they created a compilation of separate copyrighted articles when the newspaper was originally published, they hold rights to a new copyrighted work. They also claim ownership to the electronic rights in the new single, unitary work. Aware of the frequently careless treatment of stringer agreements, the media enterprises may find they have less than they would like.

A variation of programming from stringers involves the corporate "whistle blower." In order to get the *inside story*, some news media have hired corporate employees to carry hidden cameras into business meetings. The tapes of confrontations may be telecast on news magazine programs such as "60 Minutes" and "20/20." In one case, a network was caught in a novel copyright squeeze in an exposé of a grocery chain. The program included footage taped by a planted employee. The store's attorneys initially raised the issue of copyright ownership of the videotape, as well as fraud. While claims of libel are hard to sustain in light of the video proof, the grocery chain argued that since the store's employee made the tape on the job, the store was the copyright owner under the work-for-hire rule. The network's broadcast was a copyright infringement. The novel argument, however, is burdened not only by a legitimate fair use defense, but also by the argument that unless the employee's job description covered the taping of meetings, it fell outside his scope of employment. The novelty of the claim, however, suggests that copyright infringement claims may become more common in an era of video reporting.

3. Viewer's videotapes. With the minicam as ever present as the boombox, the world of stringers has expanded exponentially. In the most heralded instance of minicam exploitation, the Rodney King beating, a local television station successfully fended off a claim of copyright infringement thanks to a generous judicial interpretation. When George Holliday made his tape of the beating available to a Los Angeles television station, it arguably was expected to be for local use. He reportedly received some cash; not bad for a home movie. But no one could have predicted that the fuzzy shots would spark civil unrest, become a symbol for police brutality, and be seen around the world.

After the local airing, the television networks, and local and national news magazines, among others, clamored for copies, which were readily released. The tape achieved a level of notoriety that no other home video ever had achieved. However, while the station received on-air credit from other media, it neglected to see if it had acquired the tape with an iron-clad understanding of its rights. Its contract acquiring the tape was loosely drafted and left a loophole that inspired a copyright infringement lawsuit by Holliday. The suit was ultimately dismissed, because the judge did interpret the station's release of the tape to others to be within the understanding of the parties. The station escaped liability, but it could have avoided the issue entirely with a simple assignment or a release which more clearly covered all contemplated uses.

Any time a video is obtained from a viewer, get a release that allows the station to air the piece and disseminate it "in all medium, now existing or hereafter created." Provide credit. Pay a reasonable licensee fee, but one based on the present value of the work, not the appreciated media value. Since most minicam owners have minimal expectation that their home movies will make it big, and since the media outlet has the upper hand—it does not have to air the piece, and most minicam tapes are never seen on television—it is reasonable to obtain all useful rights for a modest sum. If the news department has the right nose for news, as our L.A. friends did with the Rodney King beating tape, it should buy all rights to the tape. If the tape has commercial or hard news value, it will be money well spent.

There are also firms in the business of tracking news events and licensing stations to use the videos they produce. One outfit in Los Angeles has a helicopter that trails traffic accidents on major thoroughfares and it licenses stations to air footage that no other camera has caught. When L.A. broke out in riots after the Rodney King verdict, the helicopter crew caught the Reginald Denny beating on tape. That video also played nationally, but for a fee. The local uses by L.A. stations were licensed; however, unlike the Rodney King footage, the helicopter entrepreneur and copyright owner captured the royalties from other media.

The contrast of these stories underlines the evolving importance and exploitations that can be made of copyrighted minicam tapes. For the media, it is urgent to appreciate that these works are not their own unless they are acquired outright. At a minimum, a license should cover whatever needs are reasonably foreseen, which should include original and repeat telecasts. In cases of special footage, it should cover eventualities that might develop, such as licensing to a network or other news outlets as an integral part of a story. If the viewer knows the value of the tape or if another station in the market prizes it more, then bidding can go up. But in the marketplace where fame is part of the coin of copyright, and where use of a name in on-air credit can be worth a lot, stations should use that as part, perhaps a substantial part, of their consideration.

4. Rip 'n read. It would be tempting for a radio station, eager to save a few bucks and still provide news and information, to deliver its hourly news headlines simply by reading the three-sentence news summaries that appear in the margins of many newspapers. This practice would push the envelope of what constitutes unprotectable facts compared with copyrighted expression. Taking more than fifteen words of someone else's news report is clearly dicey. Taking fifteen words or more from five to ten top stories of the day is even more problematic. With many news services, such as AP, Mutual, and CNN, providing news content for a price to any buyer, skimming stories off the top of a newspaper or magazine is a very questionable practice. Even though headlines are not copyrightable and quotation with attribution is appropriate in news reporting under the fair use doctrine, with the abundance of third party licensed material, undisciplined use of third party stories is legally suspect. To the extent a station wants to save on news gathering while providing listeners and viewers information, the strategy of rip 'n reading others' works without payment should be flatly rejected.

5. Frame grabbers. An analogy to rip 'n read is frame grabbing. With high tech equipment, publishable quality stills can be made from videos. A digital machine that halts action with clarity and allows prints to be made enables the video media to make works available to print publishers. The photos derived from the video, which may require some cropping or touch-up, qualify as derivative copyrighted works. Stations should pay attention to this potential source of licensing. But at the same time, they must also know the parentage of the video. If they are grabbing frames from third party videos or films, and are licensing or selling the stills, they may be violating someone else's copyright.

6. Bugs on screen. In the past five years, the news media has sought more routine ways to make indelible identification of their work product. Hence, the birth of the bug. The current practice is to run on-screen, in the lower right or left corner, a logo for the news source. This trademark branding allows a copyright owner to ensure that if video, which is relatively easy to copy and reuse, is appropriated by another, the source will be evident.

7. Titles of newscasts. "Action News" and "Eyewitness News" are among the most common titles of newscasts. Yet, each of these titles were registered trademarks, entitling the owners to assert rights against not only stations in their own markets, but throughout the country. As a matter of practice, most stations that file federal trademark registrations do so to protect their status in their local areas. Nevertheless, the rights they have secured through federal registrations are not so bounded.

The crucial point for federal trademark owners to appreciate is that if they are registered and if they learn of third party use of the same mark, they must act promptly to demand either that use cease or that it be licensed. Because broadcasting involves interstate commerce over technically wide geographic areas, the right to prevent use of the same program title in distant markets is well established. But sleeping on one's rights (in the legal term, *laches*) and allowing a third party to invest in building up a reputation transforms legal rights. Even though a broadcaster could have claimed exclusivity and stopped a use once, that right could be lost if not enforced.

The utility of enforcing federal trademark rights in the title of newscasts is made more urgent by the arrival of the Internet. It seems that many stations have local Web pages under the ubiquitous "www.(station).com." If a station has a registered trademark for the title of its newscast (Action News), it cannot only claim "www.action-news.com" but also it can prevent any other station in the country from using an identical name. (More about these Internet names in Part Four.)

8. Video monitoring. A new "clipping service" developed in the 1980s. A technological relative of the time-honored newspaper clipping service, video monitors set up shop by running a bank of VCRs, taping local and national newscasts, and selling clips to customers for a cool $125 for about five minutes of tape. Starting out as a "mom and pop" business with VCRs in the basement, the practice has grown into significant and sophisticated enterprises with national revenue in the tens of millions of dollars. Claiming that news is anyone's to take, these operations were challenged in a series of copyright lawsuits. The bottom legal line: Broadcast stations own their news programming and the video monitors need a license to reuse the tapes. This is good news for broadcasters because it is established that they can control an emerging market for focused information from their newscasts.

The principal difference between the video monitors and their newspaper clipping ancestors is that the newspaper folks buy multiple copies of a newspaper and physically clip from the copies. Under the copyright "first sale doctrine," the copies are owned by the purchaser and may be sold or given away, as long as no extra copies are made. By contrast, video monitors tape full newscasts off-the-air with commercial motivation (arguably a copyright infringement right there), and then reproduce selected portions relevant to customers. Whether they are memory tapes (copies for people who forgot to turn on their home recorder when they or relatives were interviewed on camera or appeared in a "man in the street" shot) or more sophisticated telecast researching for a company concerned about newscasts on a particular topic (e.g., Philip Morris asking for all network and Top 10 market newscasts clips discussing tobacco issues), resale of the news is a new business opportunity for media outlets.

The video monitors even fax summary reports for those who can't wait for overnight delivery of the tapes. By grabbing a few frames and running edited transcripts, a quick report can be prepared on any newscast, and it can be faxed within minutes of airing. Unless licensed by the news media, all these uses—editing video clips and texts, and frame-grabbing—constitute multiple copyright infringements.

Unquestionably, video monitoring is a secondary use of the news content. While some stations fear it will increase the potential for lawsuits, because it will be easier for third parties to spot libel or defamation when they can review tapes of live telecasts at their leisure and reflect on their content, video monitoring is here to stay. Broadcast stations and networks should assert their ownership of the content and either get into the business of selling clips or license one of the willing video monitoring firms and recoup some of their costs.

9. News management. It was not too long ago that news specialists remarked about the way in which the Soviet leaders doctored photographs to "eliminate" enemies of the State. Modern technology has only enhanced the capabilities of the media to manage news events. For example,

- During O.J. Simpson's trial, *Time* magazine was accused of darkening a photo of O.J., making him appear more sinister.
- The credibility of NBC's news magazine, "Dateline," was brought into question when it was revealed it staged an explosion of an

automobile to prove that the placement of gas tanks was a public hazard.

- And the Russians were up to their old tricks, painstakingly editing hours of tapes of President Boris Yeltsin in order to produce a three-minute speech for telecast on the eve of Russia's 1996 election.

These are but a few of the examples of facts being altered to make a point in the news. Although copyright law gives owners control over the content in their works, and technology makes it difficult to spot alterations, the news media have a special obligation. Although entertainment and opinion-oriented articles permit exaggeration, video news must maintain a standard of honesty when reporting events. It is only the public's trust that separates fact from fiction. If facts are manipulated, even though copyright law may protect the product, society suffers. It is the obligation of the news operations to guarantee that the public trust is honored.

These are a few of the highlight issues in news programming. Now let's learn about another crucial aspect of programming—music.

Chapter 14

Music Rights in Broadcasting: They're Playing Our Song

Music has a long and complex association with broadcasting and copyright law. From the earliest days, the rights to use music and the fees for those rights have been contentious. There are four crucial ways in which music and media work together:

1. **Performance.** Most fundamentally, broadcast media perform music. The radio industry is, by and large, the single largest performance outlet for music. The right to perform music on radio and television is licensed by three major performing rights societies—ASCAP, BMI, and SESAC—and a host of smaller operations and individuals that grant rights in libraries of music or individual compositions.

2. **Synchronization.** Synch rights, which involve the synchronization of music to video, are also vital to the media. Most television programming and films require merging musical components with photography. Clearing those rights, which are legally distinct from performance rights, is handled by different agents. The Harry Fox Agency is probably the best known of the group. However, many others also grant these rights.

3. **Master use license.** Once a musical performance is recorded, there is often no need to re-record the work with different musicians or orchestras. Simply use the LP, tape, or CD. However, that requires a copying of the sound recording, which is the province of the record label that made the original. The recording companies will license

the copying, but deals must be made directly with the record companies.

4. Compulsory (mechanical) license. A special provision of copyright law provides that once a musical work is published, anyone can create recordings of his own adaptation for public distribution and play on mechanical devices. The statutory procedure kicks in if a negotiated mechanical license is unavailable. The procedure must be followed and fees paid according to the rules set forth in the Copyright Act and accompanying regulations. The compulsory license may be an alternative to the mechanical license, but it requires that the media hire the artists to create the adaptation.

Let's take a closer look at these four crucial musical rights.

Performance Rights

Since the 1950s, ASCAP has labored, quite successfully, under a federal consent decree. The decree was issued because as an association of competitors, ASCAP challenged the federal antitrust law. This statute holds that *conspiracies* (read: more than two people) *in restraint of trade* (read: setting prices or requiring customers to buy or license one product, such as an unpopular song, to obtain the rights to another product, i.e., a popular song) are illegal. ASCAP, an association of thousands of songwriters, which license all the works in its repertoire on a blanket basis, fits that definition. However, the radio industry first, and later the television and cable television industries, need the economies of scale that derive from blanket licensing. What evolved is a system of licensing reviewed by a federal magistrate, who assures that the music license fee structure is reasonably fair to the composers and the users.

For radio stations, long used to performing popular or classic tunes on a 24 hour a day basis, blanket licensing of a whole repertoire makes sense. Of course, for some stations, such as all-news radio outlets, music is only a minor part of their programming, compared with the talk component. However, no station escapes the need to license the performance of music, if only to ensure that commercials with music can be aired. To fit all users, the performing rights societies have established special licensing fees for stations that have less need for the full music repertoire.

For television stations, the use of music may also be sporadic. Typically, programming sourced from the network comes with music performance rights attached. Newscasts and public affairs shows, which can occupy up to twenty-five percent of a local station's programming week, contain some, but not a predominant amount of, music. Program theme music may be licensed at the source or composed by company employees.

In general, syndicated programming creates the critical need for television station licensing. Most syndicated shows are sold to local television stations without music performance rights. However, with the proliferation of talk and game shows in daytime slots, which are the kinds of programs that contain little music other than in the theme, the need for blanket licensing has diminished. Almost twenty years ago, because the broadcast industry seemed to be paying very high music license fees, it challenged the prevailing blanket system in court. The result was the "per-program license," which was developed as an alternative to blanket fees. Let's contrast the two fee arrangements.

The blanket system allows the use of every song in the repertoire (literally a million) in exchange for a set monthly fee. Use as much or as little as you please. The fee itself is like a tax on revenue derived from programming incorporating music. As with the IRS and its Form 1040, ASCAP's and BMI's approach is to tax the revenue generated by the programming that uses music. Both advertising and program revenue, as well as barter that has quantifiable value (airline, hotel, or restaurant trades or credits; equipment leases, messenger services, you name it), is totaled, and a percentage averaging about 1.5 percent for radio and 1 percent for a television station is assessed. There are some deductibles each station is allowed to take off the top, and the adjusted revenue is calculated and the percentage applied. ASCAP and BMI routinely audit their licensees for accuracies in their reporting.

By contrast, a per-program license measures actual usage and charges fees accordingly. The per-program license involves a complicated compromise formula. The rationale of the per-program formula is that stations should pay a licensing percentage according to how much money qualified music generates. There is a cost for the privilege of opting out of the blanket fee in terms of keeping accurate records, but the effort can result in significant money savings. The formula is a bit complicated, but here is its essence.

ASCAP's per-program fee starts out with a determination of how much revenue per market the performing licensing society would be entitled to under a blanket approach and allocating that amount among the active stations in the market on a sliding scale according to ratings. To this projected blanket fee for the station, forty percent is added. This total is then multiplied by the revenue generated in qualifying programs, that is, non-network shows containing ASCAP music, and then divided by total revenue in all non-network programs. In addition, an "incidental/ambient fee" of fifteen percent of the blanket fee is tallied. This charge covers most other uses of music, including music in commercials and in news or public affairs programs. The combination is the per-program fee:

PER-PROGRAM FORMULA

- Step 1: Monthly blanket fee × 140% = A
- Step 2: A × revenues from non-network programs with ASCAP music = B
- Step 3: B ÷ total revenues from non-network programs = monthly per-program fee (C)
- Step 4: Incidental/ambient use fee: monthly blanket fee × 0.15 = D

  TOTAL PER-PROGRAM FEE: C + D

The per-program license requires that stations keep good records of music performed and revenues, with regular submissions of cue sheets and financial reports. On balance, if more than forty percent of a station's non-network programming revenue comes from programs that contain no ASCAP music, then the per-program formula will save the station money.

These individual station licenses cover non-network programs, both those that are licensed from syndicators and those that are produced locally. The performing rights societies negotiate separate contracts with the major networks for fees covering all network shows. Telecasts by the affiliates of the network programming are thus excluded from the blanket and per-program fee arrangements.

BMI has adopted its own version of the blanket and per-program fees, which it offers to all broadcast licensees. By comparison, SESAC, the much smaller European and classical music performing rights organization, typically licenses its repertoire on a fixed market fee basis. Because it lacks the pop star recordings and performances, its charges are modest. This society collects only a tiny fraction of the fees paid to ASCAP and BMI. There are a few foreign performing rights organizations, including some in Europe, that also license U.S. facilities. With licensing rights well exceeding half a billion dollars, performance revenues take a big bite out of the broadcast industry's wallet. Nevertheless, the entertainment value of music is undeniable. Just watch a movie without any music and see what you think of the experience.

Synchronization Rights

Producing original programming with music attached involves synch rights. Even though a station has a performance license, that permission does not cover the copying of music to video or film. That merger of sound and images is separately licensed.

For broadcasters and programmers, synch rights are divided into two parts:

1. Original programming. Virtually all original programming on television contains music. The theme and background music constitute integral and inseparable parts of a program. In movies, the soundtrack can be as much a selling point as the film itself. If preexisting musical recordings are being recorded onto the film or video, then synch rights must be secured. For programs that will be syndicated or licensed for network telecast, these rights are an essential part of production costs. Failure to clear these rights can wreak havoc with marketing plans.

2. Background music and incidental uses. How often does an on-the-scene telecast involve the incidental copying of music? A parade marches by and the performing band's rendition of a popular song is part and parcel of the video account. A sportscaster sums up the local team's weekly highlights by using background music to make a point. If the music were performed live and no independent copy was made, there would be no obligation to clear synch rights. The performance license would permit the rendering of the music. However, if the station composes the video with music in anticipation of telecast, or if it records the show as it is being televised live, then synch rights come into play. It is incumbent on the station to identify each composition to be used and to obtain synch rights prior to telecast. Since it is often easier to replace a song with another comparable sound before the telecast, knowing whether a piece is going to be prohibitively expensive in relation to the program's overall costs is vital at the outset.

There is one special exemption under copyright, which can be effectively used to eliminate much of the synch headache. Under the "ephemeral copy exemption," stations that hold performance licenses may use those rights to make copies of music for limited purposes. Originally conceived as a way to allow a radio station to tape music from records to smooth the transition between songs, allowing for multiple music plays in a row, rather than relying on a live needle drop, the ephemeral copy license allows for copying of music by "transmitting organizations." Those qualifying for the exemption are broadcasters licensed by music performance societies (ASCAP, BMI, and SESAC) under the blanket arrangements or any specific performing rights contract.

Under this exemption, stations can incorporate selections in any programming, provided that the use of the program is completed in six months and then is either archived or destroyed. Since stations that warehouse programming for some time may replay it years later, technical violations of the exemption are common in the industry. To date, there has not been any litigation because a station has held onto the work more than six months. Indeed, fair use may allow the retention even beyond the statutory period. However, if there is any expectation that the work will be re-aired or marketed after the six-month period, any exploitation could trigger a copyright infringement claim. Particularly as stations and networks dip into their archives and create new programs or rebroadcast old shows, determining whether all music is cleared may be the new game in town. Care should be taken with respect to any future use of these programs.

Master Use License

One of the commonly forgotten music clearance issues involves master use license rights. In part, this stems from the fact that taking musical clips from CDs is so easy, and if the synch rights have been attended to, why worry? Since 1972, however, the manufacturers of sound recordings have been entitled to a limited number of copyright rights. Prior to 1972, the companies that made the records did not own any independent copyright in their recordings. In 1972, Congress amended the Copyright Act and added sound recordings as a new category of protected works. This was done in response to rampant piracy of audiotapes. The rights granted to recording companies were limited, however, to reproduction, preparation of derivative works, and public distribution. Whenever music is taken directly from a post-1972 record, the manufacturer of the sound recording must be consulted and rights cleared.

Incidentally, these record companies have not been content with their status, as partial copyright holders. For the better part of a decade, the leading record labels have tried to persuade Congress to amend the Copyright Act to give them a performance right. In other words, although broadcast stations pay the performing rights societies, the representatives of the composer of the words and the music, and the publisher of the song sheets, they do not pay the record company that made the sound recording.

Under a recording association proposal, public performance rights would be added for owners of sound recordings; thus, all broadcasters that play musical recordings would be liable for copyright royalties to the recording companies. Needless to say, the broadcast industry has fought this concept vigorously. The stations representatives assert, "Enough is enough!" The stations make records popular and spur sales. They already pay hundreds of millions of dollars in performance royalties. Why should they pay any more?

To make the issue more palatable, the recording industry has proposed a half-step, namely, the coverage of digital sound recordings only. When broadcasters play digital works, fees would be owed to the recording company. The label representatives urge that since the digital format provides an easy way to make perfect copies, unless they are protected and compensated, digital air play will destroy the market sales of CDs. Broadcasters oppose this change as well, asserting there are technological fixes for the recording industry's dilemma, including anticopying codes that can be read by consumer machines. The issue of copy prevention and compensation will be a recurring theme in the digital environment.

Compulsory (Mechanical) License

The compulsory license is a long-established copyright principle, which permits anyone to create his own version of published music for play on mechanical devices, such as record, tape, and CD players, provided a statutory fee is paid. The compulsory license, which is used instead of a negotiated mechanical license, has three key parts:

1. **First performance by copyright owner.** The license affects only *published* music. In other words, the creator of a song is entitled to choose first release of the work. Who sings it and how it is marketed are within the absolute control of the copyright owner. This is a derivative of the copyright law's "first sale doctrine," which gives the copyright owner control over the initial public release.

2. **New arrangement must be faithful to original.** The license allows for artistic interpretation and variations, up to a point. There cannot be a significant change in the lyrics or melody under the compulsory license. Although parody—fair use—is another way to exploit a work without any clearance and make substantial changes for purposes of comment or criticism, if the compulsory license is employed, the new version must render the original in a faithful way. The variation of style is key. In some instances, a song released by one artist can become a signature piece of another. For example, although Liza Minnelli first sang "New York, New York" for the film of the same title, Frank Sinatra did his version as well. The publishers of the Sinatra recording used the compulsory license to ensure that the rights were cleared for their production. Like "Chicago," "New York, New York" is closely associated with Ol' Blue Eyes.

3. **Accounting and paying the fee.** The license requires filing a notice with the Copyright Office and paying a fee of about a penny plus per minute of playing time or about seven cents per song, whichever is greater. The fees relate only to publicly distributed copies. A report must be filed with the Copyright Office and the copyright owner, and regular follow-ups on sales figures must also be submitted. Rates can change periodically, so it is best to check on the most current rules.

Trademark also rears its head in music issues. While the easiest way to conceive of a trademark is a word or design, musical themes are also protectable as trademarks. The "N-B-C chime" is a perfect example of a musical notation that identifies the source of services. Similarly, television and radio introductory theme songs can constitute trademarks. But we must remember that a trademark is a short phrase. Therefore, it is important to develop a cogent summary of a musical theme in a handful of notes in order to gain protection as a trademark. While the full song will be copyrighted, the central lyric can be the signature sound. Programs such as "M*A*S*H" and "Seinfeld" are good examples of shows with thematic musical elements that may be protected as trademarks.

If a musical element is a trademark, it secures an additional benefit. Although copyrights last for limited times, trademarks are protectable in perpetuity, as long as they are in use and not abandoned. Themes can extend the licensing value of works well past the era when the copyrights would fall into the public domain. Since most television shows are under copyright protection, this is not an issue today. However, in the coming years, as more shows enter the public domain, even as they have continued life on new media, the trademark status of show themes will add to the value of the works.

Chapter 15

Advertising: Being Content with Commercial Content

Commercials are chock full of content rights issues. While the ads generate the money to pay the bills at all stations, broadcasters cannot be insensitive to the copyright and trademark issues contained in advertising. Sometimes, failure to attend to the logic of the law can result in heavy exposure for the stations. Commercials on radio and television fall into three types: ads presented to them by sponsors, ads they create and air for sponsors, and self-promotions.

Third Party Spots

When selling commercial time to others, stations usually receive the finished spot from the advertiser and play it in time rotations repeatedly. Since the content of these spots is given to the station by the ad agency or client, the station should require that the content of the spot already be cleared at the source. All spots from third parties should be aired only if a contract with the advertiser or the agency provides written assurance that the spot contains no infringement of copyrights, trademarks, and service marks, as well as related rights of privacy and publicity.

Nevertheless, such contractual assurances may not be sufficient to shield the station from liability. The contracts between the station and the advertiser are not binding on the copyright owner or trademark proprietor. Therefore, station personnel experienced in looking for these issues should review all spots before they air and raise questions that come to mind. For example,

- *Music:* Is there a theme used in the spot? Is it familiar? If so, has it been cleared?
- *Video:* Does the spot contain third party video? Is there a known source for it, and has it been cleared?
- *Photos:* What pictures are used in the spots? Who took them? Are there celebrities or trademarks of others that are prominent? Have the copyrights and images been authorized for this use?

The station's in-house reviewer should make certain that the spots have all vital material cleared. As publishers, stations can bear liability even if they innocently air the spot. Copyright law, for example, makes an innocent publisher liable for minimal damages of $100, even in the absence of any knowledge. More critically, these disputes can tie up personnel and run up legal bills. Forethought in the handling of spots can eliminate the potential for these undesired expenses.

Produced Spots for Others

Many broadcast licensees are blessed with marvelous production facilities. For them, the ability to produce spots for advertisers can be a significant source of extra revenue. But if a station composes the spot for the client, great care must be exercised to ensure that no copyright or trademark infringements are embedded in the commercial. Not only would the station have violated a duty to the client, but it would also bear direct liability to the owner of the works or the marks. Moreover, the opportunity for foul-ups is high because (a) the desire to please the client is great, (b) recall of third party material from available sources or archives is easy, (c) spots are often produced quickly, and (d) cutting corners helps to maximize revenue return.

Every element of a spot should be analyzed as to proper use in commercials. In-house materials available from the station's archives, from photos to video clips, may be the property of the station, but it is a separate question whether they can be used in advertising. For example, photographs taken by station personnel, which are clearly the copyrighted property of the station, may include individuals whose right of publicity could be violated if included in a commercial. A spot for a local shoe store could not use a station's photo of Ken Griffrey sliding into home, "Nike shoes up," without clearing the right with Griffrey's agent and Nike. Video obtained from a viewer who responded to a hotline request for breaking news stories should not be included in a spot without consent, even though the station purported to obtain "all rights" to the tape.

As discussed in the preceding chapter, every music note should be scrutinized for source and cleared. The use of common musical notations in commercials is a recipe for an infringement claimed. When a local department store's Christmas spot contained five bars from "Rudolph The Red Nosed Reindeer" (A song as old as the hills? Not really, it's still under copyright!), the grandson of the composer was on the telephone, threatening an infringement case. The settlement cost the station and the advertiser far more dearly than if the music had been cleared in advance.

Station Promos

Even if the station is not in the business of producing spots for advertisers, every station creates and airs its fair share of station promos. These spots contain clips of upcoming news stories, use familiar logos in contests, or associate the station personnel with events of the day. As with spots for clients, someone needs to scrutinize the content of these ads and make sure that all the elements are appropriate for inclusion. Although there is greater latitude when presenting spots for upcoming evening newscasts because the advertisements themselves are creatures of the news programming, there is no absolute safe harbor in using third party content in advertising.

Generally, the fair use doctrine is not available for commercial content. While not an absolute rule, that is a good standard to live by, because commercials can be easily shown to lie on the negative side of several of the fair use formula criteria:

- *Commercial use.* The spots start out as commercial content. Although Public Service Announcements (PSAs) are an exception, the vast majority of aired commercials are designed to generate profits for someone.
- *Substantiality.* Because spots are short, most often ranging from ten to sixty seconds, use of third party materials will be for only a fraction of the total and, therefore, will encompass a relatively modest amount of time. However, since the sponsor has a message to present, the taking of the original works of others is most often done for the fame of the original work. Thus, even though only a small percentage of a copyrighted work is involved, the taking is often substantial, the "heart of the original."

- *Economic impact.* Many copyrighted works are or could be sold for use in commercials. There is a thriving business that licenses the use of copyrighted material, including videos, photos, and music, for commercial use. Think of the widely telecast spots for U.S. Healthcare, incorporating old film footage from Laurel and Hardy, Buster Keaton, Charlie Chaplin, and others. Each video clip from these classic films must be cleared.

By contrast, there are some copyright owners who actively forswear any interest in allowing their works to appear in commercials. The composer of an inspirational theme, such as "Chariots of Fire," may simply refuse to allow the work to be licensed for commercial purposes or for certain types of products or services. Therefore, the impact on the marketplace value for the works, a key copyright test, is usually a heavy negative for the infringer.

Trademarks pose an interesting contrast in advertising. During the 1950s, the standard television spot compared advertiser products to the infamous Brand X. Wisk got out stains better than Brand X. Not surprisingly, so did Tide. No mention was made of a competitor's product name for fear that casting negative aspersions would result in a lawsuit.

Then, in the early 1970s, the FTC clarified public policy: By all means, use a competitor's trademark in the ad in order to permit useful marketplace comparisons for the consumer. However, the key is that the claims must be truthful. Paint a competitor in a false light and face assertions of trademark misuse and deceptive advertising.

This policy shift has not guaranteed that all spots are true; however, it permits Ford to say that Taurus outsells Toyota Camry and Honda Accura by 2 to 1; it allows Safeway to say its prices are lower than Ralph's or Giant's; it ensures that Channel 4 can say its newscasts are watched by twice the number of homes as Channel 7's, as long as the statements are based in truth. While some puffery creeps (others might say "charges") into advertising, the stations bear the burden of challenging claims made by advertisers that are questionable, lest they be liable for contributing to patently false claims and trademark misuse.

Chapter 16

The Olympics:
The Law of the Rings

The quadrennial quest for the gold has turned into a biannual event. With the split of the Olympic games into winter and summer now two years apart, viewers are going to be surfeited with information and advertising associated with the Olympics and the Golden Rings. Among the trademarks in the United States, the Olympic symbols have a rarefied status—they are the subject of their own special trademark statute.

Passed in 1978, the Amateur Sports Act is a special warning to the world that the Olympic symbols are trademarks not to be falsely used. The statute protects the words *Olympic, Olympiad, Citius Altius Fortius,* and the five interlocking rings, and prohibits any mark that falsely represents a connection to the U.S. Olympic Committee or the International Olympic Committee. Any unauthorized use of the marks in trade or advertising, or promotion of programming or athletic events, can be challenged by the U.S. Olympic Committee. The statute is so broad as to grant an absolute property right to the words. The U.S. Supreme Court has held that the U.S. Olympic Committee's control over *Olympic* is unlimited, even by the Lanham Act defenses to a claim of trademark infringement. The rule does not infringe the First Amendment.

While phrases like *Atlanta 96* or *Lillehammer Games* test the limits of the statute, it has been held that the *Gay Olympic Games* is a violation.

The elements of the statute are as follows:

- *Protected trademarks:* Olympics, Olympiad, Citius Altius Fortius, and the five interlocking rings
- *Prohibition:* Any unauthorized use of the marks for purpose of trade, to induce the sale of goods or services, or to promote any theatrical exhibition, athletic performance, or competition
- *Penalties:* The statute authorizes as much as $250,000 for penalties, injunctive relief, and destruction of offending material
- *Protected parties:* The International Olympic Committee and the U.S. Olympic Committee, and their licensees, have the standing to bring an action

For the media, the test of the statute comes in two key ways. First, advertising that contains Olympic symbols must be screened and aired only with confidence that the users of the Olympic trademarks hold rights. Contracts with advertisers should contain guarantees that the use is authorized.

Second, programming must be monitored. There is no prohibition on reporting events or scores relating to the Olympics. It is touchier when stations not affiliated with the network licensed to broadcast the Olympic Games try counterprogramming to attract an audience interested in the Olympics. The programming is protected by the First Amendment and may be covered by the fair use provision; however, the use must be truthful and the promos for the programming should not suggest an association with the games and a station or sponsor that does not exist.

During the 1996 Summer Games, there was much grousing by non-NBC affiliates as to how the network, which has paid billions to televise the Summer Games for many years, controlled access to events. While it is common for sports telecasts to be blacked out on non-affiliated stations, NBC took this practice one step further in 1996. It restricted access to press briefings of Olympic news-related stories. Tightly controlling media access to news developments within the Olympic Village, NBC was able to prevent the other networks from televising news stories within the confines of the Olympics.

This sparked controversy among the networks and brought charges of news management. While under copyright law and the contracts that enforce the acquisition of those rights, NBC had the legal ability to control media access to the venue and the content that emanated from it, whether it was sports or news reporting, the degree to which it limited access to public statements by Olympic officials was unprecedented.

Although doctoring photographs or staging events to recreate "actual events" is an unacceptable media practice, the isolation of news media from ongoing events raises novel concerns that may be more ethical than legal. Since copyright law facilitates control over access to the news, the degree to which other media should be restricted from unfolding events of public importance poses an important content dilemma. Does the policy supporting copyright law, which permits exclusivity in ownership of works tempered by fair use, need further recalibration? Will the legal tools at the command of the media now work against society's interests in a vigorous and competitive press? These issues will undoubtedly test the resolve of policymakers.

Copyright and access to content was not the only issue highlighted by events in Atlanta. Trademark questions also abounded. Atlanta was, by all accounts, the most commercialized Olympics ever. Licensing rights to Olympic symbols was carried to an art form by the U.S. Olympic Committee. Product categories were carved out and only a limited few, who paid handsomely for the privilege, could call themselves an "Official Sponsor of the Olympic Games."

However, that did not stop some from pushing the Amateur Sports Act to its limit. For example, although not an "official sponsor," Nike took over a warehouse just outside the Olympic Village and emblazoned it with the Nike "Swoosh." Visitors and passing camera crews would have been surprised to learn that Nike was not an authorized sponsor.

Then, too, NBC's advertising practices played a role. While Olympic sponsors had first crack at network availabilities, if any category for commercials did not sell out, they were offered to others. When product categories failed to sell out to official sponsors, spots were made available to competitors, who gleefully swooped in. As a result, MCI spots aired in time slots that the official sponsor AT&T vacated. To the national audience, the placement of MCI spots within Olympic telecasts provided the same effect as if the upstart carrier paid for the privilege of being an Olympic sponsor.

The moral of the Olympic story is pay heed to intellectual property. The "road to the gold" is paved with copyrights and trademarks.

Chapter 17

Call Signs, Slogans, Jingles, and Characters: The Bits and Pieces of Broadcasting

For broadcasters, indeed all media folks, disputes over call signs, slogans, jingles, and characters can be the most intense and important encounters with copyright or trademark law. They mark the media outlet's public persona and reputation. Since imitation of the leader is not only great flattery, but also an effective way to compete, a competitor's taking of key trademarks usually signals a strike at the heart of a broadcaster's base.

Call Sign Disputes

The FCC is the agency that grants call letter assignments. With tens of thousands of broadcast facilities, finding a combination of letters that also creates an acceptable image or theme is not always an easy task. While the FCC will assign letters to stations for new facilities on a random and arbitrary basis, stations can request preferred allocations. The key obligation is to limit call letters beginning with "W" to stations east of the Mississippi and "K" to stations west of the river. The three remaining choices among the twenty-six letters of the alphabet permit a wide variety. Many stations try to link their call sign to some theme or format. So an oldies station might go for WSGH—Solid Gold Hits; or a regional channel might apply for KGLB—Great Lakes Broadcasting.

Touchy subjects arise when two competitors in a market, whether in the same city or urban-suburban relationship, have call signs with similarity—visual, rhythmic, or phonetic. For example, WSGH and WSGA; KGLB and KGLP. Until the mid-1980s, the FCC handled these disputes. Then, in a policy statement, it indicated that it would allow the disputes to be treated like all trademark conflicts, by resort to negotiations between interested parties and filings in court, if necessary. Stations have taken up the challenge, and there have been a number of call sign disputes that have ended up in the courts. As a result, trademark rules apply to call letter disputes.

A spin-off issue involving call letters is the impact of relinquishing call signs when format or management changes. Call signs of long standing in a community may be relinquished for FCC purposes, but the issue is "who is free to pick them up?" Since call signs can be registered with the PTO as trademarks, does a change in call letters constitute abandonment for trademark purposes, allowing anyone to use the letters? This issue has never been resolved in court, but stations can do a few things to protect themselves against an arch rival taking released call letters and trying to get a competitive edge.

First of all, register call letters with the PTO. Federally registered trademarks stay on the books for up to ten years. Abandonment of trademarks requires active intent. If a station can demonstrate that even though the call sign has been released, there is still a long-standing local recollection of the phrase and a plan to use it, then it would be confusing in the community to allow an unrelated station to grab the call sign. (Exxon used this ploy to protect the mark "Humble" shortly after it consolidated all its trademarks.)

Second, maintain some actual use after the change, including such helpful notice as "WGLB, formerly WSGH." Surveys have shown that the public remembers call signs long after they cease to be used in the market. Maintaining awareness could also help diary-keepers locate the right station, even as the image of the facility is changing.

Third, sell the right to some other distant facility, or at least encourage a nonmarket station to take it over. Sometimes, call letters have a real market value for another and can be sold for a decent price. When Ted Turner converted Channel 17 into a cable superstation, he hunted around for the initials of his company, TBS, and paid a handsome sum for the call sign WTBS. Moreover, with the elimination of duopoly rules (which prohibited common ownership of several stations in one market) and the consolidation of station ownership, most dramatically evidenced by the merger of Westinghouse and CBS and its acquisition of Infinity, station owners may control dozens of radio properties, some in the same broadcast market. Swapping call signs among commonly owned stations can prevent call signs from being gobbled up by local competitors.

Slogans and Jingles

Slogans for media outlets are their key identification to the public. "News 4 You" or jingles such as, "Are You Ready For This? It's the Sports Blitz!" are prime examples of stations selling an image to their viewers or listeners. In some cases, firms in the business of developing station image packages license to subscribers the right to a slogan and related material, such as bumper stickers, video spots, jingles, on-air personalities/voices, and the like in a specific market. This means that as one travels around the country, other stations may have the same package. To the traveling public, there may seem to be a connection with the stations; however, the only link would be a common licensing source.

For stations, this permits an efficient way of capitalizing on a proven commodity. However, there are some things to keep in mind:

1. **Contracts.** As a licensee, if a station varies the slogan package it might run afoul of the contract requirements. Since a licenser of slogans, or any trademark owner for that matter, needs to maintain *quality control*, stations are not free to modify the package without prior approval. Most often, artwork, use of the marks, and other key elements may not be changed without licenser approval. Read the license contract carefully before considering modifying the package.

2. **Owning changes**. If a station develops a unique and successful edge to the licensed slogan, does it own the change? The answer to that question may not be as simple as one might expect. Look at the license agreement for starters. Even assuming a special stamp could be placed on the way the facilities use the slogan and other elements, the licenser may claim ownership of any changes under a variation of "work made for hire." Before signing on, the station may wish to modify the license agreement to ensure ownership of the elements it develops.

3. **Facilities covered.** There are often strict limits in license agreements covering the precise facilities to which they apply and the market within which they may be used. Especially for group owners,

there is no guarantee that a successful slogan can be transported to another market. Read the agreement carefully and if plans call for using Station 1 as a tester for sister facilities, make sure the agreement permits extension into other markets.

Characters

Especially in the radio business, on-air personalities create their own "shtick." Whether it is a cutesy name, an identifiable voice, or a musical interlude, there is a need for tangible identifiers that the public can associate with. Often, diary-keepers do not remember station call letters or precise time periods when they watch or listen, but they remember a key character by name. Radio listeners may not know the station's frequency, but they will remember they listened to Rush Limbaugh at 2 p.m.

In some cases, popular personalities are wooed to competitive stations. The issue that personality mobility raises is who owns the character. If we are dealing with someone's real name, absent extraordinary circumstances, the station to whom the personality defects can refer to the individual and, if desired, call the show by his or her name. There may be limited situations in which a name is so prominent that the original station might contract for exclusivity in use of the name in the market for a period of time. These agreements are disfavored because people should be free to use their own name in their chosen occupation. However, there may be a reason, such as a big upfront fee that the personality received from the original station, to justify setting a limit on what happens when he or she leaves.

In the case of fictitious names, the rules are more restrictive. Was the character or shtick developed by the personality under a work-for-hire arrangement? If so, the *employer* owns the work product of its employees and would have a right not only to prevent a defecting employee from using the fictitious name at the new station, but also to allow a replacement employee to use it at the home station. When an on-air personality known as Mr. Frank O. Pinion left one St. Louis radio facility for another, the tussle over rights to the names hit the front pages of the local newspapers. The originating station retained its rights by early contract protection. When David Letterman jumped from NBC to CBS, the fight over his Top 10 also made headlines.

It behooves all media outlets that encourage the development of themes and characters to look closely at the ownership of these properties. Particularly in an industry where people move around frequently, not just from stations within a town, but across states and the nation, defining who owns what can be difficult. If an on-air personality (DJ-1) adapts a routine made successful by another DJ (DJ-2) in a former city of employment and then he moves four states away where he uses it, who owns what? Does DJ-2 and his or her employer have a claim? You bet they do!

However, unless the preliminary work in protecting the copyright and trademark elements has been done, the rights entitlement becomes murky. DJ-2 and the employer need to have adequate proof of first use and these records may be hard to construct. Rarely are rights enforced in the situation in which DJ-1's imitations are performed in a geographically distant market. However, if DJ-1 achieves regional or national prominence, DJ-2 may gnash his teeth because he failed to act. If DJ-1 emerges in the local market, the stakes automatically become higher because ratings can be lost, and the likelihood that the dispute will intensify increases.

A few handy hints to prepare for these inevitable situations are as follows:

- Keep a checklist of the key on-air elements of the facility and rank them in order of importance.
- Determine what rights need to be secured and how: first by contract with all the participating parties, then by filing registration claims with the Copyright Office or the PTO.
- Brand intellectual property as copyrighted works or trademarks.
- For the valuable material, warn would-be infringers, no matter where they are, that you will not countenance theft of this property.
- Take action. Serve notice on the infringers and if necessary seek injunctive relief and damages under copyright, trademark, or unfair competition.

These elements are the bits and pieces of broadcasting. They are also the personality of the stations and the heart and soul of the media operation. They should not be taken for granted, because if they are, sooner or later, they will simply be taken.

Chapter 18

Colorization and Artists' Rights: Whose Work Is It?

In the mid-1980s, technology brought a marvelous capacity to movie-making. With the ability to convert film stock to digital format, changes could be made to content that appear seamless to the naked eye. Filmmaking technique pioneered in *Who Shot Roger Rabbit?* was made dramatic in *Rising Sun*, Oscar-winning in *Forrest Gump*, prehistoric in *Jurassic Park*, and totally animated in *Toy Story*. Placed in the hands of directorial masters, this technology can revolutionize programs shown on television and in movie theaters.

But the precursor and, in the view of many legendary directors, the curse of the technology, is its ability to change old films to please modern tastes. The most dramatic example of this development is the colorization of old black-and-white movies. The purpose, to make classic films palatable to the MTV generation, requires color tinting so that kids will keep the set on when classic films are shown. After Turner Entertainment bought the old MGM film library, consisting of 3,600 movies, about half in black and white, colorization had its P. T. Barnum in the person of Ted Turner. Determined to turn his newly acquired library into a stable of films for new movie channels on cable, thereby increasing product at a fraction of the cost of making new films, Ted Turner announced that the MGM classic film library was fair game for digital modification. His decision was greeted by expressions of outrage from many of the great names in moviemaking, such as Frank Capra, Jimmy Stewart, Woody Allen, and Steven Spielberg.

When first confronted with the challenge of raising their protests, the talented core of filmmakers had to understand the rules of copyright law, which the owners of movies had mastered over the years. The core of their problem is that virtually every classic film was not the solitary work of a lone individual, but rather it was the collaborative effort of scores of people—performers, writers, directors, cinematographers, producers, film editors, set designers, composers, and on and on. Take a few minutes to read the credits at the end of a movie, and you'll see how many folks it takes to create a film. Also with the credits is a notation, usually at the very end, that the producing company is the "author of the motion picture for copyright purposes."

Under the work-for-hire system, all the employees involved in making a movie, even those whose inspiration, writing, and direction created it, are contractually employed. Ownership of the work belongs to the company that pays the bills to make it. Unless the employment agreement provides otherwise, the copyright owner is allowed to change a work without regard to the interests of those whose names are attached to it. It is the rare filmmaker who has or can insist on retaining postrelease control over the final product.

At the same time that the Directors Guild of America (DGA) determined to raise public consciousness about the changes being made to classic films, which they characterized as a native American art form, the U.S. Congress was debating our joining the Berne Convention. Berne is the pre-eminent international copyright treaty, a compact that dates back to the days of Victor Hugo and the French refinement of human rights principles. Central to the heart of Berne is its Article 6*bis* and the principle of *droit moral*. Moral rights, as it is known, is the legal notion that an individual artist has the *right* to have his or her name associated with any artistic work he or she creates and to prevent alterations that harm the individual's honor or reputation.

For decades, key copyright interests, such as motion picture producers, had opposed joining Berne solely because of the moral rights clause. Its impact on their ability to exploit films was very worrisome. However, in order to stem the tide of international copyright piracy, which was costing producers over $1 billion a year, and to gain legal protections in key piracy strongholds such as Thailand and Egypt, accession to Berne became financially compelling to film producers and other copyright owners (especially software companies).

For the directors, who, along with screenwriters and cinematographers, are internationally recognized as the artistic "authors" of motion pictures, the Berne debate afforded an opportunity to put the colorization issue center stage. By going to Washington, D.C. in the late 1980s to testify, directors Woody Allen, Sidney Pollack, Milos Forman, Steven Spielberg, George Lucas, and Elliot Silverstein, forced the issue into the spotlight. Altering classic films without the permission or involvement of the artistic authors, just to fit the perceived interests of viewers, was wrong, they declared. On the other side, producer interests feared success of the protest would diminish their ability to tailor films to key markets, such as television, cable, video, and airlines, as well as newly developing digital environments. Full moral rights for artists could substantially cut the value of their film library.

The legislative debate ended with an odd result. The United States decided to join the Berne Convention, but Congress chose not to enshrine Article 6*bis* into U.S. law; rather, it concluded that "moral rights" were adequately recognized in a potpourri of American laws, including the derivative copyright right, Section 43(a) of the Lanham Act; the laws of libel, slander, privacy, and publicity; and state statutes. As an additional element of the Berne Convention compromise, Congress created the National Film Preservation Board, the function of which is to identify and honor original versions of classic American films. Classic works, selected at the pace of twenty-five films per year by the Librarian of Congress, are duly praised, but only in their original versions.

The tension that surfaced during the colorization debate between artists, whose goal is to preserve their original works, and producers, whose goal is to gain maximum economic benefit from the art, endures. Proposals to force producers to tell the public how movies have been changed when they air on television or in video formats and whether the original artists who made them object to the changes have been offered in Congress over the last few years.

Most fundamentally, the issue bears on the relationship of the medium and the faithfulness of the message to the original *artistic* concept. Although colorization is probably the most dramatic example, the relationship of technology and alteration of copyrighted film works is spotlighted by:

- *Panning and scanning*: the reduction of the aspect ratio (screen image) from the rectangular, wide screen to the square, television format
- *Time compression/time expansion*: the practice of speeding up or slowing down frame speed
- *Lexiconning*: the ability to alter pitch while changing film speed to keep the sound level constant and mask the speed changes

- *Morphing*: the technique of digitally altering video
- *Editing*: the decision to delete content for a variety of reasons, including fitting films into time slots and removing offensive words or nudity.

Recognizing that engrafting full artists' rights into the U.S. copyright system is an epochal challenge, film artists have proposed a half-step of informing the public about changes made to films by a label that would precede the telecast and would inform them how many minutes were edited out; whether the work was colorized, time compressed, morphed, or lexiconed; and whether the artistic authors (the director, cinematographer, and screenwriter) object to the changes. In response to the pressure, the studios and broadcast networks (ABC, CBS, NBC, and FOX) agreed to experiment with a modest notice to air before a televised version of a theatrically released movie. The studio's notice, which is voluntary and has applied only to network telecasts of recently released films, informs the public that films were edited to fit a time slot, formatted to fit a viewer's screen, or colorized, without further details or statement of artistic objection.

Although the producers believe this approach fulfills their obligations, a 1995 arbitration involving a FOX network telecast of a theatrical movie raises questions about the approach. When Columbia TriStar licensed the FOX network to telecast *Thunderheart*, a film about life and death on an Indian reservation, it allowed FOX to cut 22 minutes off the running time and speed up the movie by six minutes. All this was necessary to eliminate twenty-five percent of the film so it could run in a two-hour movie block of time, while permitting thirty minutes of commercials.

The film's director, Michael Apted, a noted British documentarian, saw tapes of the show and concluded the changes gravely mutilated the work. In making the movie, Apted and the screenwriter, John Fusco, had promised Native American participants that their story would be sensitively told, and that their current life on the reservation would be related. Among the scenes cut for time were those that told that vital part of the story. Apted brought an arbitration complaint against the producer and won an order that required the distributor either to carry the full notice of changes and his objection, or to replace the director's name in the credits with the pseudonym Alan Smithee. The studios chose to use the pseudonym and filed an appeal, which they lost.

Michael Apted was not the first to legally challenge alterations to his work. In the 1970s, ABC was sued by the creators of the "Monty

Python" television program, who objected when the show was severely edited for a network telecast. In a decision based on Section 43(a) of the Lanham Act, the producers prevailed in convincing the court that the altered show misrepresented their work. One of the judges even suggested that the Berne Convention's moral rights could be found embedded in Section 43(a).

As the "Monty Python" and *Thunderheart* cases demonstrate, the issue of moral rights reaches deeply into the conscience of the film-making, film distributing, and film watching communities. It foreshadows additional battles in this area. Every time a movie is panned and scanned, a photo cropped, a story edited, a tape sped up, the issues of misrepresentation of the work and of discrediting the original artists are raised. Phrased another way: Whom should the law recognize as the author of a work, and who should be entitled to control its fate in the marketplace?

Copyright is essentially an economic interest in works. Moral rights are the non-economic interests that involve individual artists and their reputations. Although motion pictures and television shows are collaborative works involving the active participation of many people, they do represent a body of work honored in our time as art. To modify these creations without regard for the artistic elements violates the interest of artists.

Alteration of art may also be decried as an alteration of history. "I Love Lucy" and "The Honeymooners" were made in black and white. That is part of their public reality. Should they be colorized because more TV sets are in color? Doing so would certainly deny their originality.

What is equally true is that the Berne Convention is playing an increasingly important role in U.S. copyright policy. Because trade in copyrighted works constitutes one of the leading export commodities of the United States and is vital to the national economy, protecting works and halting piracy through the auspices of Berne is vital to maintaining the economics of the movie and television industries. Expanding copyright protection through changes in the treaty is a major policy goal of U.S. trade negotiators in the era of digital transmissions. Finding the right balance between the economic concerns of Berne and the respect for the human element in the creation of art works will be the delicate balancing act of the coming years.

Chapter 19

Licensing and Distributing: The Business of Programming

The production and distribution of television shows and movies is a story of the business side of copyrights and trademarks. You cannot create these works, bring them to outlets, or show them to the public without appreciating how deeply these legal issues are embedded in the system. This chapter offers a short tutorial on the system.

Start with an Idea

Every program and every movie ever launched started with an idea. As you know, ideas are not protectable. A sitcom about a lower class couple that lives in the suburbs, fights a lot, has three kids, and loves pizza, or a movie about aliens racing through space to recapture a comrade and in the process destroying the world of its captors, are not substantial enough expressions to claim copyright. But take the kernel of the idea and give it more complexity (that is, detailed expression), and you move into the layer of protectability.

Flesh Out the Idea

For a movie or a TV series, "expression" usually takes the form of a treatment or proposal. Fleshing out the ideas into a story is the work of a lonely screenwriter or the effort of a small, collaborative team. Creators are often leery of showing ideas to others for fear that they may be stolen. The basic intellectual property advice is always the same: Flesh out your ideas first. Expand the notions and *write them down*. Once written, copyright law comes into play. The more refined the storyline and the characters, the more protectable they become. The early case law of copyright has discussions of protection of characters and story ideas. The key notion to be gleaned from the cases is *detail, more and more detail*.

Give Access to the Story to Others So It Can Happen

Access is another key issue. In most cases, creators need to take a risk: They must tell others about the story so it has a chance to become a rarity—the work that moves from the private world of the creator to the public world of the viewer. In any situation where one cries foul, arguing that a precious idea was stolen and used by another in a successful program, there must be a way to establish access to the original creation. Copyright law is replete with tales of people who learned the hard way when they were sued for taking a character or idea developed in an unsolicited movie script.

Protect Against Unfounded Claims

For the producer or media manager, protection against such events is essential to smooth business operations. Generally, this means taking no work on an unsolicited basis. Return unsolicited scripts *unopened*. Don't get fooled into accepting a work without a contract. Negotiate at least a short document that acknowledges that the producer owes no duty to the person disclosing the story or idea if:

- The producer has a similar idea in development independently of the submission,
- The idea or story is already in the public domain, or
- The idea or story comes to the producer from another legitimate and unrelated source.

Of course, if material is useful, be prepared to pay for the rights. Paying early is key, because early is when the producer has the most bargaining flexibility.

Who's Involved?

Sometimes an idea is pegged to a particular person's involvement. A story may come attached to a writer, director, or actor. In such a case, if the idea is a winner, the best course is to allow the principal a role but leave open the option of his replacement, if necessary. Frequently, successful concepts fall victim to egos and unworkable bargains. So anticipate the need to bring on qualified replacements for the original creators. This is a touchy topic, but one that needs to be negotiated early in the process so that the work does not fall victim to the players.

The Funnel

The process of developing television programs or movies can best be visualized as a large funnel. At the wide-open mouth, thousands, even tens of thousands, of ideas float around. As the funnel narrows, so do the number of ideas that get converted to treatments. As you might expect, few treatments make it to the script stage. While a theatrical script can be sold for $100,000 or more, and a television script for $25,000 and up, when interest is established in a script, you are at about the halfway mark in the program or filmmaking process. Getting to that point is so competitive that most folks have long since retreated and returned to other jobs.

Once a script is finished, financing for the project must be arranged. The studio system, which bankrolls projects, is the most visible and reliable source for big projects. However, independent

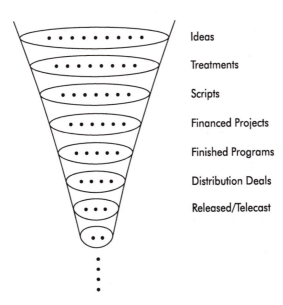

Figure 19.1 The content funnel

producers are also key players in the process. Many films and pilots are developed and paid for by someone with cash and a dream, or companies with resources and a plan. Even then, only a handful of finished programs actually get distributed and publicly released.

Among the things the creators of works, as well as the producers and the managers of the media outlets, must think about are:

- *Production costs:* What are the likely costs of making the work, which includes everything from hiring the creative team and performers to having the sound stage, microphones, and cleanup crews?
- *Clearance of rights:* What is needed to make the work, such as underlying storylines, privacy rights of individuals, music, clips, third party content?
- *Ownership:* Who owns what? Copyrights are divisible, which means that the law will separate into parts all the possible rights associated with a work. When acquiring rights, producers usually demand: "All right, title, and interest in and to the work in any medium now existing or hereafter created." It is vital that the rights are spelled out clearly in the beginning, lest there be confusion as new use is found for the works, new technology develops, or new media evolve. It is easy to make a mistake, and even the big boys slip up occasionally.

  A few years ago, when Paramount Pictures converted many of its old films to video, a song, "Merry-Go-Round," from the movie *Medium Cool*, became the object of litigation. The composer claimed Paramount had failed to acquire the video rights to his music and the use of the music in video was a violation of his copyrights. The court agreed, and Paramount had to dip into its bank account to square things up.
- *Ancillary rights:* What are the related uses or spin-off properties? Nary a major movie or television series gets produced today without a number of spin-off properties, including clothing (T-shirts, hats), music (CDs and cassettes), crosspromotions (McDonald's or Pizza Hut giveaways), kiddie goods (lunch boxes, action figures, notebooks), videos ('The Making of . . .")—you get the idea. Every one of these can be viewed in relation to the copyrights and trademarks. Ownership of those two key rights is vital to market the ancillary aspects of the works.
- *International rules:* Who controls foreign markets? As recently as the 1980s, an American film made the vast majority of its revenue

in the United States. For television series the percentage was even higher. Today, for many films less than half of their revenue comes from the domestic marketplace. It's a *global content environment* and the selling of media works is among the most important and valuable of our international trade commodities. Planning for international distribution and licensing overseas is a vital part of the business. Few works can be developed without a keen sense of the impact of international sales on the product. In some cases, international sales help define the internal content; that is, producers make the work compatible with international market needs from conception. Big budget movies that do not keep this fact of global opportunity in mind are unlikely to realize the full returns of their investment.

One international battle that has materialized involves the effort of France and other European nations to limit the percentage of a broadcast day that can be devoted to exhibition of programming originating from the United States. Motion picture distributors have protested this development, which has become part of international trade treaty discussions. Content xenophobia is clearly economically inspired. American films already dominate European theaters, and the keepers of the cultural keys want to preserve broadcast time for local products. Like most attempts at censorship, the exclusion of content based on arbitrary criteria is destined to fail; however, in the meantime, the struggle to ensure fair access to the European marketplace should remain a hot-button issue for years to come.

The Movie Distribution System

Producing works is only part of the equation. What separates the studios from the rest of the world is that they not only produce movies and television shows, they also distribute them. It is in distribution that the major revenue is realized. Although producers look to recoup their investment and make a profit, distributors take a somewhat reduced risk, hoping to hop on the joy ride when a movie breaks out of the pack. Just one or two unexpected blockbuster films can literally make a company a giant in the field. That's what happened to Miramax when *The Crying Game* grossed over $60 million at the box office, and New Line Cinema, whose *Teenage Mutant Ninja Turtles* surprised the field with over $125 million in revenue. With Miramax and New Line taking in a hefty share of those figures, they were able to break out of the pack and establish themselves in the independent film distribution marketplace.

Of course, these numbers pale in comparison with the high stakes in moviemaking and distribution as played by the studios. These companies not only pay for the making of films, but they also pay the costs of distribution and control all revenues. The average production cost of movies released by the studios ranges from $25 to $30 million, and distribution fees can be as much as $15 to $20 million. Big budget films range from $50 to $100 million in production costs, with distribution fees also rising.

An insider look at the way money is collected and accounted for in the studio system was revealed in litigation initiated by Art Buchwald, syndicated columnist, who claimed to have developed the idea for an enormously popular film, *Coming To America*, starring Eddie Murphy. The headline was that the film managed to gross $325 million but not make a profit.

How is that possible? The secret lies in the way money is raised to make movies, the hidden costs and accounting system of Hollywood, and ultimately the definition of "net profits." Here is a capsule look at the making and selling of movies.

Once a filmmaking idea takes shape, a production company (other than a studio that usually bankrolls an entire production) either covers all the costs of making a movie or it obtains gap financing—the amount that it needs to close the gap between raised funds and actual production funds. Sometimes distributors make up that gap by advancing funds in exchange for distribution rights; sometimes the money comes from other borrowed sources. Among the sources that are available is the "presale" market: Producers will presell rights to certain venues or media, such as foreign, video, or television, licensing those rights and the rewards to those marketplaces in order to raise money to make the film. Those who guess right in securing the presold markets can strike it rich, when the film becomes a hit.

The costs of production include acquisition of rights and paying all the personnel who work on the film, from directors, writers, and cinematographers, to actors, stuntmen, musicians, behind-the-scene folks, et al. (take a peek as the credits roll at the end of the movie to see all who must be paid). Thus production is the biggest need of the money chase. Finding a distributor for the film is the next key. Since many more films are produced than are released theatrically, engaging the right distributor is a highly competitive and critical task.

It is the distributor who chooses how to tell the public about a film from

- The making of a trailer (an art form in itself), to
- Where the film will open and on how many screens, to
- Promotion: the newspaper ads, television spots, talk show placements, news stories, and all.

For these efforts, the distributor usually takes several chunks of the first money in. In the case of theatrical releases, the box office revenue is split with the theater venues. On average, the division is 55 percent (distributor)/45 percent (theaters), but in practice it can range widely, from 90 percent for the distributor during the opening week, which is usually the biggest revenue-generating time, down to 30 percent in later weeks. The theaters, of course, have concession sales to compensate during the opening weeks, especially if the movie is a hit and it brings in popcorn-munching, soda-drinking, candy-eating patrons. Out of that 55 percent of gross revenue, the distributor recoups many line item costs, which are factors in defining "net profits." A close look at the revenue recoupments reveals the keys to the distributor's financial success. The biggest items are:

- Distribution fee (usually 25 to 35 percent)
- Recoupment of all payments to production (gap financing)
- Recoupment of all distribution expenses
- Interest on all money advanced
- Collateralization (recoupment) of costs from other markets, such as foreign, video, and television

When one tabulates these costs and reduces the gross, the discovery is that there is little left. When Paramount did its accounting on *Coming To America*, it kept coming up with new costs against which to play off the increasing revenue. That is how the $325 million movie *lost money!*

The Television Distribution System

Television has some important differences from theatrical film distribution. First of all, the venues are different. Television does not have a box office, so all its funds must be made from licensing fees. Second, television programming fits into two key markets: network and syndication. For network productions, the costs of production, which run about $1 million per hour ($400,000 to $500,000 per half hour), are rarely recovered from the initial network license fee. Typically, the big networks pay producers about $800,000 to $900,000 for the right to air the show on their affiliates during a fixed time slot. The networks also pay affiliates a fee for the right to program each hour of prime time and other times during the day. In exchange, the networks make their money by selling national advertising time, while allowing affiliates to keep a few minutes of network broadcast periods for local sale. It is the sale of the time, based on the ratings of the programs, that allows the networks to recoup their out-of-pocket costs. For producers, the network sales usually come with a deficit, often ten to twenty percent. The hope is that the profit will materialize in the syndication marketplace.

Syndication involves the selling of episodes of programs one station at a time, for rebroadcast over a number of years. The rule of thumb has been that a network series needs about 80 episodes to make it to syndication. With an average network run of 22 episodes a year, that means that a show needs a four-year run on a network to have a decent chance to break out in the syndication marketplace. To every rule, there are exceptions. Jackie Gleason's "The Honeymooners" is a perennial with less than half the average number of episodes.

In the 1980s, prices for syndicated product went into the stratosphere, as stations vied for a handful of popular off-network television series. Topping the list was "The Bill Cosby Show," which collected hundreds of millions of dollars in syndication fees for its first five- to seven-year run. With numbers like that, program producers saw green, and station affiliates were in a tough battle to guess what shows could help carry them in ratings battles during key off-network time slots, when stations keep most, if not all, the advertising revenue. Some shrewd station managers guessed gold when they planned their schedules. Early buyers of "M*A*S*H" paid a relatively small sum and made millions as the show's rerun popularity soared. Others guessed wrong on different shows and never recouped their long-term investment.

While the off-network syndication marketplace grew, so too did "first run syndication." Sparked by game and talk shows, this venue went from nowhere in the 1970s to the big time in the '80s and '90s. The key difference between network and first run syndication is that producers must make up all their money from the original sale of shows, many of which have little or no rerun potential. As a result, producers of these shows keep costs down and must be creative in selling their product to the marketplace. One creative selling mechanism that developed in the 1980s was *barter syndication*.

In barter, the producer fronts the costs of the production, and the station does not pay any cash for the program; rather, the station gives the syndicator a certain number of minutes of air time. Then the syndicator, patching minutes together from a hundred or more affiliates, creates a "quasi-network" of markets and sells time to advertisers for all the stations combined. In such an environment, having clearances in time periods that are attractive as well as major markets that generate large viewing is vital to the revenue chase. Unless the first run syndicator can stitch together about seventy percent of the United States households, the chances of successfully selling time to meet expenses are doubtful.

Strategic marketing can be all important. A first run syndicator may choose to roll out programs slowly in order to build a national audience. The highly successful "Sally Jesse Raphael" talk show was distributed by Multimedia Entertainment in that fashion. Developed originally as a local show on a Multimedia-owned television station in St. Louis, "Sally" was gradually released in more markets, until it built a loyal following and had affiliates in over ninety-five percent of the U.S. households.

Some successful first run syndication producers have the leverage to introduce new products. One TV distributor, King World, which reinvented the game show with programs such as "Wheel of Fortune" and "Jeopardy!" introduced "The Oprah Winfrey Show" on the basis of its success with these shows. "Oprah!," which quickly rose to the top of the talk show format, has generated hundreds of millions of dollars in profits for the producers.

Of course, with every success come many false starts. At the annual NAPTE Convention, dozens of promising pilots and first run programs are peddled, but the marketplace has little room for weakly achieving programs. As the movie funnel has a very narrow spout at the bottom of the chain, so too does the television syndication marketplace. The number of independently produced and distributed television shows that can make it is quite limited, even as the number of media outlets has increased. This is because with the movement of independent television stations to new network affiliations, such as FOX, UPN, and WB, fewer hours of the broadcast day are available for independent programs. Moreover, stations find that the competition for local viewership has shifted to news in recent years, so stations are reluctant to release time periods to syndicators when they can program local news instead.

The one bright spot in this picture has been the advent of cable channels. They have taken up some of the slack by offering new telecast opportunities for specialized programming. But cable itself is a unique marketplace, which strives to cater to niche audiences. We will discuss cable in more detail in the next chapter. What is important to keep in mind is that each venue—network, off-network, first run syndication, reruns—requires rights clearances. The savvy programmer knows that maintaining control over the properties in the expanding, but highly competitive, marketplaces is the key to success.

Part Four

Content and New Media: Cable, Satellite, Telephone, and the Internet

Chapter 20

Five Hundred Channels: A Pipe Dream

A pipe dream. Literally, a dream about transmitting programming through pipes of all sorts—cable, telephone lines, beams from outer space, even the electrical company's line into the home. The specter of new delivery mechanisms has been an enticing image for all programmers. Originally, there was fear, fear that the new media would so destroy old habits that they could bring down an industry. Did not film producers of the 1940s and 1950s worry that television would be the end of their business? Even more recently, the studios fought the advent of videocassette recorders as a threat to the sacred box office. What developed instead was an explosion of opportunity. Today, revenue from videocassette sales exceeds the take at the box office. While movies continue to draw $5 billion or so, video sales and rentals are close to $15 billion, and Blockbuster and other video stores are neighborhood fixtures.

Among cable networks, dozens cater to specialized interests in new movies, old movies, sports, nature, children's programs, sitcom reruns, music videos, country and western, art and history, Spanish language, golf, garden, courtroom hearings—the list continues. What has developed is a fragmentation of the marketplace and an expansion at the same time. Whereas two dozen years ago, the big three networks combined to rule eighty percent of the ratings—households watching programs—the percentage has shrunk to below sixty percent. What makes up the difference are a new national network, FOX, and some wanna-bes, Warner Bros. (WB) and Universal (UPN), and the host of cable networks. Folks still watch television; they just have many more choices.

In this complex offering environment, a few principles stand out:

1. Trademarks, brand names, count more than ever. In order to discriminate in a multichannel environment, people make choices most often based on familiarity. When NBC launched its first cable channel, it was coined CNBC. A later channel offering, which was formed in a venture with Microsoft, was called MSNBC. Maintaining the brand is part of the business strategy: ESPN started ESPN-2. C-SPAN begat C-SPAN2. FOX has fx and Fox News. A&E's popular "Biography" program launched an entire channel.

2. Copyright rights define market entitlements. All too soon, some folks who believe they have rights to programs in all media, in all markets, learn that may not be the case. It has already been mentioned that the composer of music to the song "Merry-Go-Round" thwarted Paramount's effort to convert the film to videocassette without checking on rights. In the medium of cable, satellite, telephone, and cyberspace, similar questions can be asked. Since rights are divisible into infinitesimal parts, absent ownership of rights "in all medium now existing and hereafter created," questions can materialize as to who can exploit a work in the emerging markets.

3. Spin-offs and sequels are part of the game. For television series, it's the spin-off. Establishing a popular program, endearing characters, or social themes can result in spin-off shows. "Mary Tyler Moore" begot "Rhoda," and "The Cosby Show" led to "A Different World." In films, it's the sequel: *Terminator, Terminator 2; Alien, Aliens, Alien*[3]. To capitalize on success requires planning. It is not enough to hold the rights to the expression in the initial work. Derivative works, which may evolve from plot, characters, or theme, are part of the mosaic. To maintain hold on the work and all the fruits of that labor requires knowledge of copyrights and trademarks.

Establishing cable channels, one of the new games in town, means starting with an idea, refining it into a viable niche, tying down programming, and selling, selling, selling. It took more than three years for the creators of the Sci-Fi Channel to put together such a plan. One essential ingredient was claiming trademark rights to the title. With the establishment of "intent to use" (ITU) rules, it is possible to apply for a name of a channel years before launch.

A key problem cable channel originators face is that a descriptive title will not be allowed as an ITU. Since many new networks have very descriptive titles, such as The Golf Channel or The Game Channel, applying for a trademark on an ITU basis may be foiled by the Trademark Examiners, who reject intent-to-use applications for descriptive marks.

It is useful to bear in mind that it takes roughly a year to process a trademark filing, and with good counsel on your side, the time can be strung out even longer, if necessary to permit actual use. In the meantime, if some use can be made of the title, then a "use-based claim" may be substituted. But since highly descriptive marks require secondary meaning, which is acquired after a campaign targeting public awareness and expending a healthy advertising budget, it remains a roll of the dice to secure protection for the descriptive title of niche channel. That fact also explains why some channel ideas face stiff competition and similar-sounding names, such as Talk TV, The Talk Channel, and America's Talking.

To cover one's bets, it may be desirable to link a channel to an established market participant. Successful magazines are viewed as a top source for new channel titles. The House and Garden Channel is a prototype of taking a magazine and extending the line to cable programming. CNN's Sport Channel, CNNSI, is a coventure with *Sports Illustrated*.

Another route is to take popular marks and extend the brand. We've already mentioned NBC and CNBC. MSNBC merges two powerhouse marks in Microsoft and NBC. Turner Entertainment used its logo as the basis for Turner Classic Movies—TCM Channel, while CNN extended its franchise when it established CNN Headline News. Disney's launch of The Disney Channel was a natural because of its established credibility.

Aside from a logo, lining up programming rights is critical. A cable channel may begin as a two-hour segment on another facility or an independent operation with about six hours a day of original programming. By *original*, we don't mean brand new, because the staple of many channels is reruns, reruns, and more reruns. But with six hours of programs a day, repeated three to four times, a full channel can be born.

In most cases, programming costs are pegged pretty low, lest the channel consume itself before establishing a loyal audience. It takes three to five years and some breaks to lock a channel into a large enough public awareness to make a go of it. With sixty million plus cable homes (about two-thirds of the off-the-air marketplace), survival (being able to charge for subscribers or have enough eyeballs for advertisers) translates into no less than ten million households and preferably more.

In the tough world of cable access, cutting deals with the leaders of the cable marketplace, companies such as TCI, Time-Warner, Comcast, and Cox, is a fact of life. Being available on their systems is the answer to the cable channel creator's dream. But the price of access can be high. Often, the originator of an idea sells large chunks of it to those who can help advance the ball. Discovery's largest shareholders are cable giants TCI, Cox, and New Channels.

TCI secured a big stake in Turner Entertainment (WTBS, CNN, CNN Headline News, TMC, and the Cartoon Channel), gained during a period of TBS vulnerability in the 1980s, which was spurred by Turner's rapid expansion, expensive acquisitions, high startup costs, and cash shortages.

Even being on systems serving ten million homes or more is not a guarantee. It has been suggested that while the public watches more television today, an individual viewer's loyalty is limited to about eight to ten channels. Tops in the group are the networks, and usually a leading independent signal and public television station. That accounts for more than half the public's viewing. Most of the balance comes from a handful of other specialized program categories: movies, sports, news, sitcom reruns, children's programming, and arts or nature. This leaves very little room to attract a large enough loyal following.

To move past competitors in the race for public attention requires more than clever marketing. Events or circumstances may catapult a channel into public awareness. For CNN, it was the Gulf War and O.J.'s trial. O.J. also put Court TV on the map.

In its early development, Discovery's business plan had a crucial programming feature—cheap programs. It was able to acquire rights to hours and hours of science programming for a very low price. The content owners parted with their property, which was otherwise gathering dust, for a bargain price. This enabled the channel to offer a varied schedule, as well as a clear market identity.

Building the different ingredients of his cable network came dearly to Ted Turner. One of the visionaries of the medium, Turner literally invented the cable superstation by taking a downtrodden UHF station based in Atlanta, changing its call letters, and making it available to cable systems around the United States. At the time, cable served the primary purpose of making fuzzy pictures clear. In 1972, FCC rule changes opened up the possibility of extending cable. However, it was not until Turner offered WTBS to systems nationwide (and others who relayed WGN, Chicago and WOR-TV, New York) that the relatively small cable industry (serving twenty percent of television households) got a big boost. It was Turner's acquisition of the Atlanta Braves baseball team and his movie packages that converted his sleepy UHF into an attractive programming alternative.

The satellite delivery of the three superstations provided the first new offerings directly for cable. The arrival of Home Box Office (HBO) in the latter part of the 1970s, and ESPN in the early eighties, gave cable a marketing advantage compared with traditional broadcast stations. Access to first run movies, live sporting events, and the superstations, provided the public a reason to subscribe—programming alternatives to the networks. By the end of the 1980s, dozens of cable channels were established and cable subscriptions exceeded fifty percent of all television households. For some, channel overload was taking hold, but thanks to the remote control device, speedy access to the myriad of choices was easy.

Yet, as cable gained in popularity, the marketplace changed. The costs of developing new channels skyrocketed to tens of millions of dollars. Copyright and FCC rule changes destabilized cable's financial picture and new competitors emerged from satellites in outer space and from telephone wires into the home.

Fast on the heels of cable's development, the satellite resale industry established itself as a competitor to cable. With the advent of home dishes, receiving units that could take signals directly off the air and bring them into the home, eliminating the need for cable hookups, the number of players in the marketplace expanded. As digital technology advanced, direct broadcast satellite (DBS) systems bypassed cable and served the home viewer directly. DBS became viable as the number of channel offerings increased, the size of the receiving dishes shrank, and the ability to offer crystal-clear signals became technically feasible. With hundreds of channels of programming floating around space, gaining access to as many of them as possible became the obsession of many home owners.

The newest players in the programming puzzle are the telephone companies. With a transmission line into the home and technical capacity to deliver video as well as voice communications, telephone companies, the Baby Bells, and their cohorts, are perceived as the next big player in the video marketplace. FCC rule changes, which allow a video dial tone, make it legally feasible for the phone companies' wires to serve as program pipes. Creating relationships that encourage consumers to obtain television programs from these traditional common carriers will require marketing skills and manipulation of expectations. But it is happening. In the next decade, the delivery systems will be open to more players.

Chapter 21

Compulsory Licensing: Government's Helping Hand

A central part of the success of the cable industry was the creation of the compulsory licensing scheme. This copyright policy compromise was essential in the formulation of cable as a big time player in the media market.

To understand the tension in the compulsory license scheme, a brief bit of history is instructive. In two important copyright cases in the 1960s and 1970s, the U.S. Supreme Court held that under the Copyright Act of 1909, cable companies had no copyright liability to program sources. During those days, cable principally retransmitted FCC-licensed broadcast stations. The Court ruled that the cable operators were just like their subscribers; they were on the "viewer side of the equation." Since "viewing" did not violate an exclusive right of copyright owners (go back and check Chapter 3 if you disagree), there was no liability for the system operators with regard to the copyright interests when they delivered signals to subscribers.

These decisions caused a firestorm reaction in the programming community. In an era when cable television served less than twenty percent of U.S. television households, the medium was considered by some of its most vociferous critics as a "parasite" on the broadcast community's very being. The local television stations paid hefty fees to acquire programs, and cable operators freely took those signals and made a buck, simply by delivering them, unchanged but with a clearer picture, to households in the market.

When the FCC changed its rules in 1972 to allow cable operators to bring in distant signals (New York City stations to Albany, Pittsburgh, or New England), local broadcasters were screaming. Not only was cable taking the product of the broadcaster and making a buck, but it was also draining audiences from local affiliates without any legal obligations. The criticism mounted and reached reconciliation in Section 111 of the Copyright Act of 1976, The Limitation on Rights: The Cable Compulsory License. This compulsory license has five main elements.

Cable's Duty to Pay Programming Sources

The compulsory system recognizes that cable systems owe a copyright duty to owners of content. That duty is satisfied by paying a required fee for the *retransmission of distant, non-network programming*. The fees were originally set by statute and are subject to revision every five years by negotiated settlement between copyright owners and cable operators or by Congress' designated agent. In the absence of a negotiated reallocation of fees, first the Copyright Royalty Tribunal (CRT), a federal agency created by the 1976 Act to manage compulsory licensing, and beginning in 1994, the Library of Congress, is authorized to revise the fees in a rate-making proceeding. In addition, because the original fees were based on FCC rules in place when the Copyright Act was passed in 1976, any material changes to those 1976 FCC rules expanding the scope of retransmission rights could also trigger royalty changes.

In fact, three such rule changes have triggered important alterations of royalty rates. When the FCC eliminated its *leapfrogging rules* (limits on which signals could be imported by cable operators) and *syndicated exclusivity (syndex) rules* (blackout standards that required cable operators to delete programs on distant signals that duplicated shows to which local television stations held exclusive market rights), rate changes were ordered by the CRT. In addition to per-channel rates, the CRT imposed a charge of 3.75 percent of cable revenues for each newly imported signal that would have been prohibited by the old leapfrog rules. Then, because cable operators were freed of the obligation to black out duplicated programming, the syndex surcharge, which boosted fees about twenty percent, was added as well. When the FCC reinstated syndicated exclusivity in 1990, the CRT canceled the surcharge.

A term in the Copyright Act, DSE, standing for "Distant Signal Equivalent," is the basic unit of cable royalty calculations. Independent signals are credited with a DSE value of one and distant network and educational signals a value of one quarter (.25). The cable systems tabulate DSE based on signal carriage and pay fees according to a sliding scale. Due to the shifting nature of channel carriage (signals are added or dropped periodically), blackout considerations, and partial carriage rights, among other things, the calculation of royalties can become very complex. Even the proper definition of a cable system and the question of community borders affect calculations. No one should attempt to determine the fees owed without a detailed secondary transmission manual at one's side.

Local and National Network Signals Are Free to Cable

The compulsory license mandates that cable subscribers are entitled to receive local programming and national network programming free of any copyright charge. The winning argument was that when cable acts as a mere conduit of programming that is otherwise available off the air, only aiding in reception by boosting signal strength, no copyright fees are due. Also, the legislators reasoned that national communications policy was advanced by ensuring that all U.S. households had access to the national networks, ABC, NBC, and CBS. With the arrival of new networks, such as FOX, WB, and UPN, the definition of network is being tested, but for the time being only the big three are free under the compulsory scheme.

Intermediary Conduits, Including Telephone Companies and Satellite Resale Carriers, Pay No Fee and Have No Liability

A corollary of the "mere conduit" rule applies to telephone companies and satellite resale carriers that serve as middlemen, delivering programming to cable systems. When the copyright rules were developed, cable was an earth-bound system. Signals were picked up off the air by system operators or by common carriers and retransmitted from the originating broadcasting station through a relay system of point-to-point microwave towers placed on tall buildings or mountain tops to the cable systems' headends (central signal processing centers). The cable operator then delivered the signal into subscribers' homes by coaxial cable or wire. Although the terrestrial microwave links were instrumental in getting the signals to the system, they did not serve subscribers directly and made no change to program content. Because of this status, they were exempted from any copyright liability. Similarly, telephone companies whose facilities were used to deliver signals to any part of the cable system's infrastructure were defined as exempt under the compulsory copyright rules.

When Ted Turner, then owner of a struggling UHF station, WTBS, Channel 17 in Atlanta, looked at the compulsory scheme, he saw an opportunity to take his channel and make it available beyond Atlanta. At the same time, satellite transmission of broadcast signals—the microwave relay in the sky—had just become a reality. By uplinking WTBS to a stationary satellite 23,000 miles above earth, when the signal was relayed back down, it could be received everywhere in the U.S.!

This remarkable accomplishment was spurred on by a regulatory change approved by the FCC—the elimination of the leapfrog rules. These rules limited the signals that cable operators could "import" into their service area by requiring that a closer channel be given preference over a more distant signal. When the leapfrog rules were terminated in the late 1970s, this meant that cable systems could bring in a distant signal from anywhere in the country without regard to geography.

The rule change led Turner and a few others to capitalize on a provision of the compulsory scheme that was developed with the old terrestrial and telephone technology in mind. Under Section 111(a)(3) of the Copyright Act, a retransmitter that merely facilitated the delivery of signals to cable operators was exempt from any copyright liability. The resale carriers were viewed like truckers consigned to pick up the programming from one place (say, Atlanta) and deliver it to another place (say, L.A.). When the FCC dropped the leapfrog rules, a critical barrier to Turner's vision was eliminated. Within a few years, WTBS became a nationally distributed cable channel (along with WGN, Chicago, and WOR-TV, New York) and the cable superstation was born.

The popularity of these signals did much to get cable into new homes. With the availability of programming on these channels that was different or complementary to that available on local stations and the networks, television viewers saw a reason to subscribe to cable—more video choices. The attractiveness of cable increased as these superstation outlets became sources of unique programming. In the 1980s, Turner and his growing companies bought sports teams such as the Atlanta Braves and the Atlanta Hawks and programming such as the MGM Film Library. This latter acquisition, which cost over $1 billion, gave Turner over 3,600 classic movies to use in developing programming choices on his expanding cable network empire.

While the compulsory license does not apply at all to the host of nonbroadcast channels that have developed during the past decade (movie channels such as HBO, Showtime, Cinemax, and The Movie Channel; sports channels such as ESPN and Home Team Sports; variety channels such as Discovery, The Family Channel, Nickelodeon, fx, SciFi, USA, Lifetime, and dozens of others), it was the ability to deliver something different at the time (the distant off-the-air independent signals) that put cable on the map for good.

Royalty Distribution

Since its inception, the compulsory royalty scheme has generated several billion dollars for programming interests. The money is paid by cable systems filing twice yearly one of three forms created by the Copyright Office. Form 3 is for the larger cable operators and looks like a complex version of the IRS's 1040. Medium-sized systems file an abbreviated Form 2, and tiny operators, with less than $300,000 in annual revenue, submit Form 1, and pay a fixed fee of about $60.

During 1978, the first year of the compulsory scheme, only about $10 million was collected. However, with the growth of cable subscriptions, from twenty percent of TV households in the early 1970s to almost two thirds of all television households in 1996, the royalty pool has multiplied dramatically to almost $200 million. This bounty is divided among a core of avid claimant interests in hotly contested royalty proceedings. The principal interests have been:

- Program suppliers: film and syndicated programming distributors (first run and off-network)
- Joint sports claimants: Major League Baseball, the National Hockey League, the National Basketball Association, collegiate sporting interests, and other sports programmers:
    - Commercial television stations
    - Public television stations
    - Music performing right societies
    - Religious programming owners
    - Canadian broadcast interests
    - National Public Radio

When the CRT was abolished in 1994, the victim of a lethargic administrative system and a Congress looking to shave costs, the royalty distribution responsibilities were transferred to the Librarian of Congress, with the mandate to empanel Copyright Arbitration Royalty Panels (CARPs). The procedure requires the CARP to conduct a hearing and to issue a report to the Librarian. The Librarian may accept or modify the recommendations of the CARP. Any final decision may be appealed to the U.S. Court of Appeals for the District of Columbia.

Following the rulings of the CRT, the first CARP recommendation and the Librarian's ultimate decision awarded the majority of the royalties to program suppliers, the film and television syndication industry. However, following a recent trend, the percentage award to the program suppliers dropped from almost three quarters to slightly over one half. The biggest gainer during that period has been sports interests, whose share has risen from about fifteen percent to almost thirty percent. This reflects the strong influence of sporting events on cable subscriptions. The remaining share of royalties is split among the parties: commercial television receives about 7.5 percent, music performing rights societies 4.5 percent, public television 4 percent, and religious programmers and Canadian broadcasters about 1 percent each. National Public Radio (NPR) has been gifted 0.18 percent by the parties, who have settled on an award for noncommercial radio, even though it was decided in the first royalty case that commercial radio stations were not entitled to any compulsory royalties.

Cable Prohibited from Altering Programming

At the center of the compulsory scheme, which allowed the cable industry to "get movin'" by making otherwise inaccessible programming available, was the precept that cable operators could not alter content or sell ads during retransmitted programming. The statute makes very clear that with regard to retransmitted signals, there can be no alteration of programming or substitution of commercials by the cable operator. The local and distant signals must be carried in their entirety, without change for the compulsory scheme to apply.

This makes good policy, but it has been tested by new syndicated exclusivity rules. In 1990, after years studying commercial television's complaint about loss of market share to retransmitted, distant signals, the FCC reinstated the right of local broadcasters to demand that a program on a distant signal be deleted if the local station held an exclusive right to air the program in its market. Initially, only one superstation, WTBS, Atlanta, had a "syndex-proof" signal; that is, it had national broadcast rights to all its programs. The other two primary superstations, WGN, Chicago and WWOR-TV, New York carried programs that local stations could force cable operators to delete. That created a real dilemma for many cable operators, who wanted to continue to deliver to subscribers these popular stations, but who did not want the hassle of deleting and substituting programs, or worse, carrying a blank channel. Such a situation would wreak havoc with the orderly scheduling of programs, could impose a heavy administrative burden, and could turn subscribers off.

To answer the problem, clever satellite resellers, firms in the business of picking up the broadcast signals off-the-air and relaying them to cable via the satellite, took advantage of a loophole interpretation of the compulsory licensing scheme. When WTBS became almost universally available on tens of millions of cable households, Turner sought to capitalize on the national reach and sell advertising on a national basis. Obviously, the charges for spot ads for a national cable audience of a million or more would greatly exceed the rates for a local Atlanta independent seen by only tens of thousands of viewers. To manage this two-tiered system, Turner developed a local ad rate for Atlanta-only and a national cable rate. It then arranged with the satellite reseller to substitute commercials before the signal was uploaded on the satellite. Because the substitution was done by order of the television station, and not the cable operator or the satellite company, it did not run afoul of the compulsory license. And the U.S. Court of Appeals for the Eighth Circuit so ruled.

With that decision in hand, enterprising satellite resellers moved to solve the syndex dilemma, which was even more complicated than the goal of achieving a split advertising system. By taking the WGN and WWOR-TV signals and substituting programming at the uplink site, the carriers were able to qualify for the compulsory scheme when the local regular WGN and WWOR-TV programming aired. And when the syndex-plagued programming arrived, they substituted programs for which they acquired national rights. This activity rejuvenated many old programs unseen for years, such as "The Jack Benny Show" and the "Lawrence Welk Show." In the intervening years, the cable superstations, relying on the advertising advantage of reaching millions of cable subscribers, cleared their own facilities to contain more syndex-proof programming.

There was another twist for the satellite resale carriers that led to another compulsory scheme in copyright law. Since the satellite retransmitted signal is available everywhere in the United States and since most channels of cable programming migrated to satellite retransmission as the preferred mechanism for delivery, an industry selling huge satellite receiving dishes directly to home owners burgeoned in the 1980s. The dish sellers offered people the ability to get cable programming without paying the monthly cable fees. Simply buy the dish and point it to the satellite. Without cable hookups, one could download all programming "from the bird." The practice also had appeal to restaurants, bars, and motels, which saw a cheap way (once the dish was paid for) to deliver programming to customers.

Needless to say, the practice created copyright controversy. To grab hold of the issue, Congress passed a compulsory license just for home dish owners. Under the scheme, noncable private homes using satellite receiving equipment could be licensed by satellite resale carriers to receive FCC-licensed broadcast signals. The carriers are obligated to collect royalties from the homes and to pay them into a pool, also managed by the CRT and the Library of Congress.

The Satellite Home Viewer Act (SHVA) created a second compulsory system in 1988. While the amount of money generated by the SHVA is relatively small compared with the compulsory license (annual royalties equal about $4 to 5 million), the system has enabled many underserved television households in "white areas" (places where no off-the-air broadcast signals can be received and no cable exists) to benefit from local and national programming. The royalty rates are modest, so many families find the investment in the equipment worth the effort. The law and the implementing regulations are complex, including limitations designed to prevent the satellite reseller from taking distant network channels and collecting fees from local home owners, if the home owner's community is not a "white area," so a careful review of its details may be required in special cases. One word of caution! This compulsory system applies only to broadcast signals, *not* to any of the specialty cable channels like HBO, ESPN, Disney, or CNN.

Intense controversy has developed, however, because the satellite compulsory system does not cover commercial establishments, such as bars, restaurants, and motels. These businesses want easy access to the satellite programming. Concerned about the high fees associated with retransmission, many establishments resist paying top dollar rates and try to opt into the SHVA scheme. However, no broadcast station and no satellite carrier can authorize retransmission of programming owned by another, even though they have the right to deliver the content locally. The Copyright Act construes these for-profit uses, such as attracting customers to a sports TV bar, as requiring direct licenses. They are usually available from the channel owner, even though they may be more expensive to secure than under the compulsory license.

A related battleground is the entitlement of new players, such as telephone companies, to the compulsory license. If the Baby Bells and other telephone operators are to compete on an even playing field with the cable systems for viewers, they must have access to the compulsory royalty scheme. Otherwise, they would have to reduce offerings to subscribers who like particular broadcast channels. As could be anticipated, denying access to the compulsory license could leave the phone companies hopelessly behind in the race to secure viewers.

The Copyright Office has requested comments on whether the phone companies qualify for the compulsory license. If it turns out they are denied participation, expect legal appeals and pleas to Congress. The compulsory scheme is part of the body and soul of cable. While it is an artificial marketplace that does not have many content-owning advocates, it was a helping hand at a formative time for cable and remains a force that has been essential to cable's rise in public popularity. Denying rights to the emerging media would place a potentially insurmountable barrier on the road to their success. Look for the compulsory scheme to apply evenhandedly to all new media.

Chapter 22

Media Consolidation: Content Synergy

Mergers and alliances have been the code words for the nineties in relation to content and the media. Foremost, the cost of content has driven parties together. It is so expensive to fill up a broadcast day with attractive content that unaffiliated players can rarely accomplish the feat. Furthermore, there is a desire to leverage the goodwill that comes from public associations in one market with another. For that matter, trademarks, which brand content or pipelines, provide an important lever in the swing to secure the loyalty of viewers.

In the 1980s, borrowing money was easy, whether in the form of direct loans from banking sources or public financing in the form of junk bonds. Some folks, chief among them Ted Turner, expanded their base accordingly. By the mid-1980s, Turner's cable strategy was paying off. WTBS was established in over ninety percent of the cable homes, and cable was reaching half of total U.S. households. This meant that his local station in Atlanta had access to forty-five percent of all U.S. homes, more than any single station in the nation by a large multiple. To attract viewers so he could leverage the access into advertising return, Turner needed content. He approached the two big content markets—sports and movies. He acquired sports franchises in baseball and basketball. Then, he bought a movie library. By the mid-1980s, WTBS was spending over $25 million a year in license fees for telecast rights. He needed more programs because he was competing not just against Atlanta stations, but against the national networks and local independent stations throughout the country. The need coalesced into his bold decision—to buy the MGM Studio and Film Library. It represented the richest lode of moviemaking, over 3,600 films, including classic works like *Gone With the Wind* and *Casablanca*, and perhaps the greatest American movie, *Citizen Kane*. The net cost was $1 billion after Turner sold off the MGM studio and lot. To fund this programming appetite, Turner sold "junk bonds" on Wall Street. He became so indebted that he was also forced to turn part of the control of his business over to the cable companies that carried his channels, including the largest cable operator, TCI.

The purchase of the library, later complemented by acquisition of the RKO library, turned Turner Entertainment into one of the great treasuries of film, which it used to expand its place in the cable marketplace. Turner launched new movie channels, Turner Network Television (TNT) and Turner Classic Movies (TCM). He became a catalyst for controversy by colorizing many of the 1,800 classic black-and-white films in the MGM library, remaking them in his vision, so they would be palatable to the MTV generation.

Ironically, Turner's success brought him into the target range of other players, bigger players, in the media marketplace. While he lusted after CBS (making an offer for the company in the 1980s), Turner built CNN and other news networks. In 1995, Turner proposed a merger with Time-Warner. The publishing and film conglomerates of Time and Warner Brothers, which took about a decade to bring their own merger of disparate cultures and resources into a unified whole, planned the next ultimate merger of content-based industries. Because the concentration of content was so substantial, the FTC and the Department of Justice very carefully reviewed the impact of the merger on the information and media marketplace. In the end, those agencies signed off on the deal, which placed under one roof more content-based properties than has ever been owned by a single source.

This acquisition, however, is in keeping with two trends. One is the rapid consolidation of media entities during the last five years: Viacom buying Paramount and Blockbuster; Disney acquiring ABC-CapCities; Westinghouse taking over CBS. The other is the movement toward alliances, such as Microsoft and NBC, various Baby Bells, FOX and TCI, and all kinds of software firms with programmers and distributors.

These trends reflect another reality: The world, not just the U.S., is the media marketplace. To compete on the world stage, the chief players need to assemble sufficient resources. Without the strength that comes from consolidations and alliances, there is a belief that the players will not stand a chance as leveraged operations based in Europe and the Far East rise in strength.

There is no question that the leadership of American companies has created a new look in the international content marketplace. With new technologies and modes of communication emerging, most notably the Internet and satellite, it is urgent that major players have a global strategy for developing content and marketing it. This does not mean there is not room for individuals. In fact, it remains a truism that the individuals who are able to create visionary works can succeed and, indeed, can succeed on an international scale. The creators of the Home Shopping Channel, for example, succeeded in defining a programming niche of international appeal. They walked away from their creation with great wealth.

Yet, it remains a fact that the most impressive linkage has always been and will be strong content with universal means of distribution—the studio system grown up, the moviemakers and movie distributors, the broadcast programmers and broadcast networks. In the 1970s, the broadcast combination created by the networks was so powerful and such a barrier to entry that the big three broadcast networks were prohibited from syndicating programming that originally aired on their facilities. Viacom, itself a media powerhouse, was born from the rib of CBS, as the source of CBS-produced programming that CBS could not legally syndicate.

As the 1990s draw to a close, the networks have been allowed back into the business of syndication by an FCC that concluded that the programming industry no longer needs regulatory protection. Inspired by the concern that off-network programming tends to dominate the syndication marketplace and that the broadcasting networks could, by controlling original network release, artificially preclude third parties from marketing syndicated programming, the Financial Syndication (FinSyn) Rules restricted the networks for almost thirty years. It was the elimination of the FinSyn that inspired the mergers of Disney and ABC and CBS and Westinghouse. Combinations of program producers and distribution networks, which always make sense, now dominate network broadcasting.

To bring the movement full circle, we now turn to the newest media, the world of the Internet. In this interactive marketplace, old content issues are being challenged by the very force of technology.

Chapter 23

Cyberspace: The Code of the Wild West Revisited

It seems as if in the past few years, technology has been changing so fast that it is hard to imagine a set of rules that could bind the marketplace. Indeed, the discovery of the Internet as a friendly environment by hackers and scientists has given way to its becoming the newest mass media. Tens of millions of people have learned the ease of turning on and tuning into the information explosion. Even some politicians have been known to sing its praises.

The promise of the Internet—the code word for interconnected networks, including the special one that is run by complex rules established by the U.S. Government—can be summarized very briefly: It enables anyone to be a publisher.

Unlike every other mass medium, for which a hefty investment in infrastructure is required and for which only the investor is able to control content, the Internet and its related on-line service companions, demand only minimal commitment of resources. A serviceable computer, a modem, and a service connect can cost less than $2,000 and can permit any user to interact with others. With software that enables e-mail or by establishing an Internet address (domain name), anyone can communicate with a broad universe. The nature of those communications has been the focus of tense copyright debate in the past few years.

The essence of the debate is that many users of cyberspace publish copyrighted materials belonging to others. It might be a popular software program, it might be a famous picture, it might be a story or article, it might even be an entire book or the latest CD by a popular musical group. But work by work, copyrighted materials are being posted around the world, for the public to read, view, or enjoy, without clearance or permission from the copyright owner. This is causing real consternation in the copyright-owning camps because works are being exploited and markets diminished without any accountability.

The matter is made more crucial because the technology of the computer, the digital transformation of words and images to zeros and ones that can be read and understood by machines, enables copying to be done with amazing success and clarity. Unlike the wizardry of video and audio cassette recordings or the trusty photocopy machine, digital copies perfectly reproduce the original. When CDs are replicated by computers, they sound as true as the ones you buy in the store.

This means that copying becomes more precise. It is also easy. Pushing one letter on the keypad can download and store all the data at one's command. In copyright parlance, we have:

- A *transmission*: from the host server or computer, via telephone lines or other transmission circuits, to the receiving unit
- A *copying*: when the work is stored on the receiving computer and also printed out
- A *display*: when it is visually seen on the monitor
- A *performance*: if there are speakers that translate the sounds

These activities constitute one of the greatest challenges to effective policing of copyrights. The content industry is very concerned that the attitude of users of the Internet, which is bolstered by an early image of "anything and everything goes" and of sharing information for free, will render their published works unmarketable. After all, if you can locate the text on-line, why go to a store and buy it?

But buried in the technology itself are some solutions. Prime among them is *encryption*. The content owners are moving quickly to establish parameters by which content can be coded so that access to it will be denied unless the user's activity has been approved. In other words, pay per use. In addition to encryption, other high tech solutions, such as creating a *digital signature*, which would have to be displayed before one could access data, or *anticopying codes*, which would prohibit downloading before it starts, will play a role.

The battle over cyberspace content is playing out in several venues. First, in the courts. There have been a handful of lawsuits that mark some of the important principles of ownership of works. In general, courts have been willing to apply copyright law to the Internet. Thus, a hacker who uploaded software so that thousands of his nearest and dearest could benefit from the works was held to be an infringer. Even more compelling, the on-line service that promoted the transactions as a way of popularizing its services also was held accountable.

That ruling sent shivers down the spines of many on-line service providers, because the ability to permit access to the many and varied Internet sites was now in question. When a different court held that the service provider was not responsible for every text transmitted by it, a sigh of relief was heard throughout the industry.

The posting of copyrighted works of the Church of Scientology gave birth to a series of lawsuits testing whether it was fair use for a disgruntled disciple to allow the public access to the closely guarded texts, and for the *Washington Post* to print portions that it was able to retrieve. In two equally defensible, but seemingly inconsistent, rulings, the same court held the disciple liable for copyright infringement, but the newspaper qualified as a fair user.

It is important to note that these early decisions in the media law of cyberspace apply only in the jurisdictions where they operate. Unless Congress revises copyright law or the U.S. Supreme Court issues an opinion, many of these issues may not be truly resolved. Especially in light of the international nature of the transmissions, no single lower court can be said to offer the definitive treatment of works in the new media.

While the courts have been trying to digest the relevance of the new technology to older laws, the U.S. Government, inspired by its baby boomer leaders, has proposed a "modest tailoring" of the copyright suit to fit the new fashion of the Internet. In a report entitled "Intellectual Property and the National Information Infrastructure: The Report of the Working Group on Intellectual Property Rights," known as the *White Paper* for short, the Department of Commerce summarized many of the developments associated with the "information superhighway" and urged some limited copyright reforms.

Chief among the recommendations was a proposal to amend the Copyright Act's definition of "distribution" to include "transmission." While many legal scholars believe the distribution right already encompasses all transmissions, the Working Group was convinced that saying it clearly would make the point more forcefully. Other key proposals of the Working Group included:

- Creating a Copyright Management Information System, intended to make copyright ownership and other information relevant to users not only readily apparent, but also unalterable by users
- Prohibiting any device that defeats anticopying or encryption technology
- Granting a performance right in sound recordings
- Permitting libraries and the visually impaired increased rights with regard to digital works

Far from being perceived as modest tailoring, the *White Paper* provoked a strong outcry from many quarters, who read the report as seriously undermining the balance of the copyright system. Most notably, the *White Paper*'s treatment of fair use was attacked. Even though the Working Group created a series of meetings, known as the Conference on Fair Use (CONFU), to consider if reform was needed, the absence of a strong reaffirmation of the fair use standard and the encouragement of "pay for play" technology was perceived as a diminution of rights. A coalition of companies in the hardware, software, telecommunications, and educational industries challenged the suggestion that the limited change to the definition of distribution was desired.

Among the most contentious issues that has arisen in the development of cyberspace is that of "service provider liability." In the *White Paper*, the Working Group indicated that it favors current legal rulings, which have held service providers responsible as contributory infringers for the activities of users or subscribers when they send or receive the transmissions without copyright clearance. However, the on-line service provider industry—which includes commercial service firms such as America Online, Prodigy, and CompuServe; telephone companies; thousands of Internet connectors; and educational institutions from pre-K to postgraduate—objected strenuously.

They posited that there was no practical way in which they could monitor the bits of information in the billions of transmissions occurring over their systems and know whether the works were copyright clean. Moreover, thanks to remarkable "hot key" technology, which allows the computer user to move efficiently from site to site, accessing distant databases at the click of a mouse, there is no way that the service provider can discern whether the hot-key sources included works without clearance from the copyright owner. The bits of data do not reveal what content they contain until displayed on a receiving machine, and even then there is no apparent signal that the works have been licensed or not.

If the service providers are held accountable, the true culprit—the remote computer owner—could avoid liability altogether because such persons are difficult, if not impossible, to identify. Moreover, the scope of potential liability (actual damages from lost sales or statutory damages of $500 to $20,000 per work) could create liability on so massive a scale as to put many providers out of business.

The dispute between content owners, who know that many prized copyrighted works, including popular music, videos, texts, and photos, are being disseminated around the world without clearance, and the service providers, landed in Congress' lap in early 1996. By organizing a series of negotiating sessions among interested players, Congressional leaders discovered the depth of the dispute.

A potential solution that surfaced in negotiations was the idea that if a content owner notifies the service provider that it has good reason to believe that a particular site contains infringing material, the service provider could voluntarily block access to the site or remove the site from its system, thereby avoiding any claim that it was a contributory copyright infringer. The broad outline of the "take down" solution seemed to satisfy some, but not all, of the service providers; educators, in particular, worried that a mandatory takedown approach could harm their ability to use copyrighted works in teaching.

Of equal concern was how to treat those service providers who were "mere conduits." If a service provider was merely making a connection for a subscriber and had no involvement whatsoever in the content, should there be any responsibility at all? Like the satellite resale carrier exemption in the case of cable retransmissions, or the phone company when it comes to a question of liability for telephone conversations, it was argued that the mere conduit should bear no copyright duty to the content owner.

While the principle is easy to state, defining it in statutory language proved more complicated. If a service provider offered subscribers special software or hot-key menus, did that transform the activity from mere conduit to contributory infringer? What if the service provider believed, as many educators asserted, that the subscribers' use was covered by the fair use exemption? Equally important, how could the service provider know what the content is and meet its obligation to respect privacy, as required by other federal law?

Finally, should the take-down system be mandatory? Should the content owners be denied the right to sue service providers for copyright infringement until they make the take-down request? The owners steadfastly insisted they should not be obligated to give up the right to surprise any infringer with a lawsuit. However, they suggested that if a voluntary system were established, they would eagerly embrace it.

With so many questions, the service provider liability issue, along with the other recommendations of the *White Paper*, passed into the legislative black hole. It will be revisited in the coming years, when all these issues will have their chance to be aired again.

Chapter 24

Trademarks and the Internet: What's in a Name?

To the world, it seemed as if the Internet, that interconnected tangle of thousands of networks and millions of host computers, was born one day in 1993 or 1994. Even Microsoft Master Bill Gates ignored it until then. By the mid-1990s, from daily news stories to hot stock offerings, a new mass medium arrived.

But in truth, the Internet's roots date back several decades. Started as a U.S. government plan to coordinate super computers, it extended to university research institutions and their networks. When the means of sending graphic images was designed, it turned public. In its early days some enterprising hackers took advantage of public ignorance, adopting famous names as their own. That action had a trademark corollary that reverberated years later, as we shall see.

Now the Internet's commercial potential is being plumbed in every corner of the globe. As the Internet technology ushers in a new era of mass communication—with emphasis on *mass*—the single most critical ingredient in finding one's way along this information highway is knowing the sources of data you want to locate. While copyright law guides the use of content, trademark law provides the means by which the sources of the content are properly identified and the commercial reputations respected. To understand the importance of trademarks for this new medium, let's take a quick Internet trademark tutorial.

The Address System of the Internet

In its early decades, the Internet's defining feature was a complex routing system. Interconnected networks were identifiable by a unique string of numbers or names. Today, the Internet contains thousands of computer networks and millions of "host" computers that share information. Locating a network and communicating with a specific computer on that network is the electronic equivalent of sending a letter to a specific address somewhere in the world. The task of establishing electronic mailing addresses (domain names) is regulated by national voluntary organizations. In the United States, the Internet Network Information Center (InterNIC), an organization funded by the U.S. National Science Foundation and managed by Network Solutions, Inc. of Herndon, Virginia, performs the function. In Europe the task is coordinated by RIPENCC and in Asia by APNIC.

Domain Names

A *domain name* is a unique combination of letters, numbers, and dashes that routes packets of information among computer users. The domain name consists of both the arbitrary identifier chosen by the Internet user and a generic abbreviation that categorizes users (e.g., ".com" for commercial, ".edu" for educational institutions, ".gov" for U.S. government agencies, ".org" for organization, ".mil" for US military, and ".net" for network). To locate an individual at an organization, a clause (including a person's name and the symbol "@") precedes the arbitrary identifier. Combining all the elements, the address and name would read:

john_smith@cbs.com

To obtain a domain name, one contacts InterNIC, (at "hostmaster@internic.net"). The World Wide Web, a popular part of the Internet that is user friendly and capable of transmitting pictures as well as text, is identified after the @ sign as www.

InterNIC requires a domain name applicant to have at least two computers (servers) and an e-mail address that connects it to the Internet. The connection can be made directly by the applicant or through an Internet Service Provider. A list of qualified service providers may be obtained by fax from InterNIC. The service provider may also request the domain name on your behalf. In either event, it takes several weeks for the request to be processed. InterNIC grants domain names on a "first come, first served" basis. And, oh yes, no two sites can have identical names. When a computer user reaches the domain site, it is common for a *home page* to appear on-screen. A home page has an introductory screen, which includes a table of contents, identifying the information that can be accessed by the computer user.

With the explosion of interest in domain names, InterNIC became swamped by requests. To meet the new burdens placed on the system, Network Solutions changed its "no fee" policy in 1995. To acquire a domain site, a $50 fee is due; an annual $50 charge will maintain it. If a service provider makes the request on behalf of the applicant, it may assess its own fee.

Domain Names May Be Used Like Trademarks

While Internet addresses are not trademarks per se, domain names function as a source of identification, much like a telephone number. Some telephone numbers, like 1-800-AMERICAN, 1-800-MATTRES and 1-800-BLUEBOOK, have been held protectable as trademarks.

As a general proposition, in order for a trademark to be protected in commerce and registered with the PTO, it must be *affixed* to a good or label and *used* in commerce. Placing a mark on a box or other consumer item sold to the public or incorporated in advertising is sufficient. But what about cyberspace communications? The U.S. Trademark Office has said that a mark displayed on a computer screen is acceptable as evidence of use. Thus, displaying logos on a computer screen establishes trademark rights. Since the PTO will register on-screen identifications when used in connection with the provision of services, domain names and their related home pages may also serve as marks for the viewing public.

Trademark Disputes Flourish on the Internet

When famous marks are used as arbitrary identifiers, trademark conflicts arise. Recently, there has been a spate of Internet trademark litigation. One case involved use of the name "kaplan" (famed for SAT review courses) by arch-competitor Princeton Review, Inc. (PRI). Although the registration of "kaplan.com" by PRI was allegedly a prank, the dispute over its use reached the courts and arbitration. In addition to taking its name for the competitor's address, Kaplan accused PRI of "urg[ing] prospective customers to e-mail 'KAPLAN horror stories' to us at kaplan.sucks@review.com."

For its part, PRI claimed registration of "kaplan.com" broke no law, nor rule of Internet. Its objective was to create an electronic brochure and to comment on its competitor. The arbitration panel found for Kaplan and forced PRI to relinquish the name.

Kaplan and PRI were not alone. Although initially only a small fraction of the Fortune 500 had claimed their name as an Internet address, as businesses woke up to the importance of Internet sites, parties began fighting to protect their name, including:

- *MTV:* The cable service challenged a former employee, a VJ (Video Jockey), who registered "mtv.com" as *his* Internet address to promote music services related to his work for MTV. In the case, which was subsequently settled, the VJ asserted that he used the name with full knowledge and permission of MTV, after MTV saw no need for the address identifier.
- *Better Business Bureau:* In a case filed in federal court in Kansas City, Missouri, the Better Business Bureau claimed that the assignment "bbb.com" and "bbb.org" to Clark Publishing violated its long established trademark rights.
- *Knowledgenet:* Another trademark complaint involved Knowledgenet, Inc., an IBM subsidiary, against Boone and Co., which requested and was assigned "knowledgenet.com" for computer-related services, a business already occupied by the plaintiff. In an additional twist, Knowledgenet named Network Solutions as a codefendant, asserting that its role in assigning the domain name without consideration of trademark law made it contributorily liable.

In response to the trend to assert trademark rights in domain names and to prevent its becoming embroiled in trademark disputes, Network Solutions propounded a new domain name policy in July 1995: When anyone seeks a domain name, it will have to affirm that it has the right to use the mark for interactive purposes and that if a dispute arises, it will indemnify and hold Network Solutions harmless from any claims.

Further, if a *registered* trademark owner challenges a domain name assignment, the party to whom the name was assigned must justify its use. Failure to satisfy InterNIC may result in the domain name being withheld. If an objecting party is not registered but has trademark rights, and if the dispute cannot be equitably resolved, InterNIC may withdraw the name assignment and await a court order or arbitration decision.

In announcing this policy shift, Network Solutions made clear that it did not believe it had any legal obligation to evaluate trademark rights before making domain name assignments, nor did it have the resources to conduct responsible trademark searches. It believed the domain name assignment process would be unduly burdened by any such effort, increasing costs and materially delaying name assignments.

Nevertheless, as an entity making such allocations, Network Solutions may find it difficult to extricate itself from the trademark morass. Although this policy shift is a reasonable effort at transferring responsibility to the affected parties, until Internet naming policies are widely understood, and businesses and individuals pay sufficient attention to them, disputes will continue to flourish and the naming organization may be called into account for its actions.

What's more, after Network Solutions imposed the $50 annual fee on Internet users, it created itself into a $40 million business overnight. The firm became so flush with cash that it even developed a plan to "go public."

Trademarks on the Internet: Legal Quicksand

Trademarks on the Internet is legal quicksand for other reasons as well. While famous brand proprietors may have a strong claim to ownership of unique words, those whose mark is known in a narrow specialty, such as Kaplan, may find their trademarks claimed by similarly named but unrelated parties, if not total strangers. Because domain names are granted exclusively and nationally, the trademark principle of "concurrent use" cannot apply in cyberspace.

A related issue is name depletion. Since there can be but one address "kaplan.com," the list of available names can be quickly allocated, forcing firms desirous of using a specific name to seek alternatives. Although simply adding one letter, for example, skaplan, creates an entirely *different* domain site, it may not relieve the trademark problem of likelihood of confusion as to cyberspace sources. Consider the InterNIC revised naming policy. Network Solutions will recognize the trademark rights of identical, registered marks. To the extent that marks are similar but not identical, or relate to products or services in different lines of commerce, applying the policy will be difficult, if not impossible.

Another issue waiting in the wings is that of trade dress protection for computer screen images. The "look and feel" questions, which have been analyzed in copyright infringement claims, have a trademark corollary. With the U.S. Supreme Court holding that trade dress and color are entitled to trademark protection, creators of computer screen images may look to protect their display images and screen colors. Core questions raised when seeking to protect screen images will be whether the screen images are functional, whether they establish a distinctive visual impression, and whether they have achieved secondary meaning.

In what may be deemed the ultimate irony, the Corporation for National Research Initiatives (CNRI) and the Internet Society, non-profit groups organized to promote the Internet and the national information infrastructure, are locked in a dispute at the U.S. Trademark Office with Internet, Inc., owner of the MOST automated teller network, over the registration of "Internet" for banking and publishing services.

In 1989, before the word became publicly synonymous with the international computer network, the PTO granted Internet, Inc.'s application to register "Internet" for automated banking services. Prior to the passing of the five-year incontestability period, CNRI and Internet Society applied to cancel registrations of the mark and opposed six new filings. At the same time, the opposers had filed their own applications for registration of "Internet Society" for publishing. Internet, Inc. has opposed that filing. As with other TTAB litigation, a final decision may be years away. In the meantime, hundreds of trademark applications seeking to register marks that include the word Internet are on hold.

The Geography of the Internet and Trademarks

Another important trademark phenomenon of the Internet is its international aspect. Electronic communications are not bound by traditional geographic considerations. Because the Internet can be accessed with the touch of a keypad and because it stretches across oceans to foreign lands, trademark proprietors find that the territorial integrity of their marks may be breached.

Although traditional trademark law allows different trademark proprietors in New York and Florida to use the same mark, on the Internet defending exclusive geographic zones in a digital world is difficult. People can communicate as readily with colleagues or customers in the same building as with those residing thousands of miles away in foreign countries.

The degree to which trademarks relating to new services on the global information superhighway will be protected is unclear. The subject of defining new services is before experts of the World Intellectual Property Organization (WIPO), as they consider amendments to international trademark treaties. The Commerce Department's *White Paper* also recommends that international classifications be updated to reflect new goods or services offered in cyberspace.

Transborder communications, whether across state lines or nations, also raise the legal issues of jurisdiction and choice of law. For example, is an Internet user liable to be sued anywhere its home page can be displayed? When cases arise, whose governing law applies—the jurisdiction where the transmission originates or where the transmission is received? In one decision, a California couple that operated an "adult" bulletin board was found guilty of transmitting obscenity via interstate telephone lines under Tennessee law and sentenced to several years in prison. In another case, a New York court dismissed a trademark suit against a Missouri business because its only contact with New York was the fact that its home page could be accessed online. For trademark owners and users, it will become a "must" to pay greater attention to the details of laws they would normally ignore.

Chapter 25

Conclusion

We have crossed a divide, from an era of media that directed content at the public into the era of interactive communications in which the public reshapes the content, from broadcasting to interactive digital communications. In an age marked by new means of transmitting data and information, the definition of legal rights to content will be tested as never before. Content will be exploited without consent in ways that traditionalists will abhor. An effort to bring order and reason to the new medium is being met with a countervailing cry: Copyright Is Dead! Internet guru Esther Dyson surmises that content cannot be protected, so why try? Turn it over to the wolves and earn your living selling ancillary goods and services—a bleak specter for those who believe in the regime of content developed over our history and whose livelihood is based on that system remaining in place a few more years.

The chances of copyright or trademark law, for that matter, dying as the millennium draws to a close is apocryphal. True, there is concern about how to protect rights, how to stop unauthorized copying in an age of wonderfully easy copy machinery. But that does not mean the system does not have technical fixes and legal solutions. Rather, as the century closes we face the challenge of instilling in a literate electorate a new appreciation for the values that underlie the faith—a belief that the fruits of intellect deserve society's respect, its praise, and its protection.

Index